SOMERSET CRICKET

A post-war Who's Who

David Foot & Ivan Ponting

REDCLIFFE
Bristol

ACKNOWLEDGEMENTS

THE AUTHORS: DAVID FOOT has followed Somerset Cricket for more than half a century, writing about it in newspapers and magazines for much of that time as well as penning a number of acclaimed books on the subject. He also covers other sports, was a drama critic for The Guardian for more than 20 years and has worked in radio and television. IVAN PONTING has also spent a lot of time peering at Somerset cricketers over the boundary rope. He, too, writes books, but until now they have all been about football. The two of them share a love of Somerset, the county of their birth.

The authors would like to thank the following: Peter Robinson, the Somerset coach and former player; Eric Hill; Gerry Brooke, Paula Crook and the rest of the Bristol United Press library staff; Andy Cowie and all at Colorsport; George Baker, Barry Hugman, Hugh Watts and Mike Tarr for help with pictures; John Dowell for his splendid design; Maggie Rugg for exemplary typesetting; John and Clara Sansom of Redcliffe Press; Colin Bateman; Pat, Rosie and Joe Ponting, a proof-reading team extraordinaire.

Illustrations: the main suppliers were Bristol United Press and Colorsport, with significant contributions from George Baker and David Foot. The picture of John Cameron came courtesy of the artist, Mike Tarr.

Cover photos, clockwise from top left —
Front: Viv Richards, Harold Gimblett, Mark Lathwell, Ian Botham
Back: Brian Close, Andrew Caddick, Bill Alley, Maurice Tremlett

Designed and typeset by Interface (0395) 68681

First published in 1993 by Redcliffe Press Limited, 49 Park Street, Bristol BS1 5NT

© David Foot and Ivan Ponting

ISBN 1 872971 23 7

British Cataloguing-in-Publication Data. A catalogue record for this book is available from the British Library.

Printed by The Longdunn Press Ltd, Bristol

EXPLANATORY NOTE: The entries in this book are arranged in roughly alphabetical order, with some variations to account for considerations of design and layout. Abbreviations used in the statistical notes at the end of each entry are as follows: SFC: Somerset first-class matches. GC: Gillette Cup. NWT: NatWest Trophy. BHC: Benson and Hedges Cup. SL: Sunday League. LOI: Limited-overs internationals. RHB: right-hand bat. LHB: left-hand bat. RF: right-arm fast bowler. RFM: right-arm fast-medium. RMF: right-arm medium-fast. RM: right-arm medium. RSM: right-arm slow-medium. OB: off-break bowler (right-arm). LBG: leg-break and googly bowler (right-arm). LF: left-arm fast. LFM: left-arm fast-medium. LMF: left-arm medium-fast. LM: left-arm medium. SLA: slow left-arm. WK: wicketkeeper. HS: highest score. BB: best bowling analysis for innings. HT (following entries on runs or wickets): highest total in season. 0 wickets signifies the player did bowl but without success; where there is no mention of wickets he did not bowl at all. MoM: Gillette Cup/NatWest Trophy man of the match award. GA: Benson and Hedges gold award. * denotes not out. Statistics refer to Somerset careers only.

INTRODUCTION

John Arlott was in no doubt about it. Somerset was his second-favourite county, not far behind the beloved native Hampshire. Taunton was one of his spiritual homes. He loved the countless quirks of history; he loved the Dickensian inkwells (now sadly gone) up in the little, precarious press box where metaphors, jokes and battered foreheads from dipping ceiling beams were shared. Arlott knew all the names: erstwhile secretaries of autocratic bearing, and obscure amateurs whose cricketing prowess was at times as perplexing as the so-called rationale of their selection in the first place.

In 1975, when the county were celebrating one of their centenaries, the Bard of Basingstoke was asked to come down and be interviewed for a TV documentary. The first question was put to him and he was away. He reeled off a comprehensive index of Somerset players from the earliest days. There were evocative stories about almost all of them and vivid descriptions of their eccentricities. Arlott had a wonderful memory, quite apart from a poetic turn of phrase. Anyone would have thought he had come from Stogumber or Stoke St Gregory. The television director kept the camera running, mesmerised as he was by the enchanting verbal output. It was John who suddenly broke off. "I think it's time for refreshment," he announced.

He led the startled film crew to the boot of his car. Claret was magically produced, uncorked and passed round. Then Arlott returned, unwaveringly professional as ever, to the identical spot where he had been reminiscing to the camera. "Let me see," he said in that distinctive burr, "where was I? Oh yes, I was talking about Sammy Woods, wasn't I. We'll start that sentence again. You can start rolling whenever you like."

His affection for Somerset was shared by many, of course. Robertson-Glasgow, wooed west in the first place by John Daniell, was blissfully happy when playing for the county. It was unthinkable, he used to say, that he might have played for any other. He may have been a man of scholarship but the humanity of a cricket field, enlivened by badinage on the third-man boundary, gave him breadth and infinite joy.

Somerset's popularity is something of a paradox. They have never won the championship, although they have come third five times. Until 1979 there wasn't even a trophy to be seen. In the early years and mid-1950s they propped up the table four years running. They were back there again in 1969, 1985 and 1991.

But this is not a book about records and statistics. Instead it is about the *people* who made up the teams. Some had individual brilliance and represented their countries with distinction. There were the honest craftsmen-professionals. Some came down from the North, just like the Geordie Test player Arnold Fothergill did in Victorian times, the marvellous, underrated Ernie Robson much later, and others like Ellis Robinson in the early 1950s.

Every player who represented Somerset since the war is included in these pages. Some made no more than a single appearance and we are left to wonder whether they were ever asked again. Indeed, should some of them have been in the first place? Such speculation is part of the charm, frequently infuriating, of Somerset. The pen-portraits are apt to touch on character, the flavour of the man, rather than dally on their deeds at the wicket.

The hope is that names, in some cases almost forgotten, will revive warm and evocative memories. Once more, the reader is left quietly to chuckle at the enforced multi-captaincy policy of 1948 or at those hoary jibes that Somserset were nothing less than a 'League of Nations'.

Here we can again look back reflectively on some of the wonderful pros who dominated the late 1940s and early 1950s: Gimblett, Wellard, Buse, Lee, Hazell, Tremlett and Stephenson. Or memorable overseas players like Wight, Alley, Greg Chappell and McCool. Or ponder anew the contributions of Langford, Kitchen, Virgin and Ken Palmer. Or dwell with a warm glow on the seasons when Rose was the leader, while Richards, Garner and Botham brought glamour to the West Country.

The book is an exercise in nostalgia. But is is hoped that it will also stimulate debate — as we consider again the influence of Brian Close who arrived, disenchanted with Yorkshire, to shake things up at Taunton in the early 1970s; as we agonise once more over fragile and flawed temperaments, and lost opportunities. Above all, this is a human record of considerable affection, spanning nearly half a century, through to the years when Lathwell and Caddick brought Somerset recognition again, and daydreams were rekindled.

David Foot, September 1993.

BILL ALLEY   1957 - 1968

Yes, of course, the craggy old leg-side spellbinder should have played for Australia. He was pencilled in for the 1948 tour of this country and would almost certainly have come, but for a ghastly accident in the nets when his jaw was broken. It coincided, more or less, with domestic bereavements. His Test aspirations were over; he came to Lancashire to play league cricket instead.

And from there, at the age of 38 (as far as one can calculate) this tough, streetwise ex-pug from Sydney surprised everyone by turning to rural Somerset. Very soon he was one of them down there; rolling a lethal ball in the skittle alleys, going out with his 12-bore, following the hounds. He also played his cricket, noisily and never less than entertainingly. He was not once going to be inhibited by convention and accepted style at the crease. He was made for the partisans and not the poets.

Bill had the unfailing eyes of a country fox. He picked up the flight of the ball quickly — and belted, this sturdy left-hander, in the rough direction of mid-wicket. Legside fielders knew it was coming but rarely stood the chance of a catch. He pulled and hooked with immense power and total disregard for the coaching manual. But the repertoire was wider than you thought. Many of his runs came from pugnacious chops to third man. He could produce, at times out of sheer mischief, an exquisite cover drive.

This cussed old campaigner took 134 and 95 off the Australians at Taunton. In that extraordinary 1961 summer he scored more than 3,000 runs. He never stopped smiting — or talking. Some said he spoke his mind too much, that he belly-ached too much. But he could also be, in that anti-establishment way of his, a most amusing companion. The crowds, not just in the West Country, loved him. In addition he was the meanest of exponents of medium-paced swing and seam, while no-one remembers him putting down a catch at gully. Later, as a top umpire, his popularity was sustained, even among batsmen who were victims of his propensity for the LBW decision.

Bill became in spirit a Somerset man. Yet he resented the fact that the captaincy eluded him, despite promises, and that a small group of pros, upset that he had dropped Langford when standing in as skipper, seemed to have ganged up against him. He was equally resentful over the imposed conditions that led to his departure. The old welterweight bristled for a long time. Yet what a tonic he had been. *Photo opposite.*

WILLIAM EDWARD ALLEY Born Sydney, Australia, 3.2.19. LHB, RM. Cap 1957. Acting Captain 1964. SFC: 350 matches; 16644 runs @ 30.48; 24 centuries; HS 221* v Warwickshire, Nuneaton, 1961; 1000 runs 10 times; HT 2761 in 1961; Double — once in 1962; 738 wickets @ 22.04; BB 8-65 v Surrey, Oval, 1962; 100 wickets once; HT 112 in 1962. GC: 16 matches; 281 runs @ 20.07; 25 wickets @ 16.20; MoM 3. New South Wales, Australia, 1945-48. Fc umpire 1969-84.

LES ANGELL   1947 - 1956

Older villagers at Norton St Philip, with an affection for cricket, were almost as quietly proud of this local boy as they were of their famous and ancient inn, The George. As a club batsman for Lansdown, Les was as prolific as he was unassuming. When he arrived at Somerset, he was never quite going to establish himself in the way of predecessor Frank Lee. He was neat, correct and perhaps a trifle too wary as he countered the new-ball men at county level. He was rightly in awe of his opening partner, Gimblett (though just once he dared to outscore him) and in his less diffident moments could pull out a few exquisite cover drives of his own. Team-mates were delighted when the popular player got his hundred — against the Pakistan tourists.

FREDERICK LESLIE ANGELL Born Norton St Philip, Somerset, 29.6.22. RHB. Cap 1950. SFC: 132 matches; 4596 runs @ 19.15; 1 century; HS 114 v Pakistanis, Taunton, 1954; 1000 runs once; HT 1125 in 1954; 0 wickets.

Les Angell

BILL ANDREWS — 1930 - 1947

The county never had a more impetuous devotee. He took on successive secretaries and committee members. He said his piece — with stammer and unequivocal fervour. At times he was regretting it afterwards. Apart from the starchier elements within the club ("that bloody barrack room lawyer, Andrews . . ."), the county was soon embracing him again. He loved Somerset with an undimmed passion and although fired four times — twice as a player and twice as a coach — kept coming back for more. Some would argue that he was the greatest character Somerset ever had. His funeral, complete with lurking TV cameras and hundreds of admirers, was that of a celebrity — just as Sammy Woods' had been before the war.

As a cricketer, one recalls him inevitably in tandem with his great friend, Arthur Wellard. Bill bowled the inswingers, so well in fact that he took 100 wickets four seasons in succession. It is possible that he would have played for England but for the war. He had a theory that Wally Hammond vetoed his chance. Twice he completed the double, so was no mean all-rounder. At least he played for an England XI in festival matches.

Few equalled the sheer range of his cricket. His claims that he played professionally also in Wales and Scotland are well documented. He played in the leagues, in Minor Counties, and was finally back captaining his beloved Weston. And, whatever the snubs, he was always around to offer the county advice. Bill was a marvellous coach of schoolboys, in particular. Many, according to him, were potential Len Huttons; all were affected by his undiluted zest for the game. He spoke at hundreds of village cricket dinners. He told hundreds of stories, the majority of which were endearingly slanderous. He could exasperate but was also much loved by all who shared his unbridled instincts for the game. For someone so gregarious, it was sad to note the reclusive nature that went with depression in his late years. *Photo opposite.*

WILLIAM HARRY RUSSELL ANDREWS Born Swindon, Wiltshire, 14.4.08. RHB, RFM. Cap pre-war. SFC: 226 matches; 4833 runs @ 15.59; HS 80 v Lancashire, Old Trafford, 1937; 1000 runs twice; HT 1141 in 1937; Double — twice in 1937, 1938; 750 wickets @ 23.39; BB 8-12 v Surrey, Oval, 1937; 100 wickets 4 times; HT 143 in 1937. Died 9.1.89.

JON ATKINSON — 1985 - 1990

The Somerset debut, at Weston, couldn't have been more romantic. He arrived at Clarence Park to watch the match with Northants — and found he was playing. His name wasn't even on the scorecard. But his parents were there to applaud, and so from the other end of the wicket did Botham. Atkinson, just 17, showed not a flicker of nerves as he hit three sixes and 11 fours in a handsome, intrepid innings of 79. It gave false hopes. He continued to strike the ball well, but less consistently. His bowling lost some of the control shown in schooldays. He captained Cambridge and really had enough talent to come up with a better playing record. Was he inhibited, sub-consciously, by the presence of his dad Colin, a captain and president of the club?

JONATHON COLIN MARK ATKINSON Born Butleigh, Somerset, 10.7.68. RHB, RMF. SFC: 14 matches; 422 runs @ 28.13; HS 79 v Northamptonshire, Weston-super-Mare, 1985 (debut); HT 184 in 1989; 4 wickets @ 107.00; BB 2-80 v Indians, Taunton, 1986. NWT: 1 match; 1 wicket at 16.00. SL: 7 matches; 85 runs at 17.00. Cambridge 1988-90.

Jon Atkinson

COLIN ATKINSON 1960 - 1967

The rare distinction of being captain, chairman and president of the county club reflected, in his case, intelligence and integrity — and a surprising determination for a shy and self-deprecating man. His cricket could be as competitive as anything you'd expect from a North Countryman. But he also had to work with dogged resolve to make himself into a better player than he naturally was.

He arrived at Millfield in 1960 to teach, with the promise that he could have the summer off for cricket if Somerset wanted him. Harold Stephenson, who shared the same geographical roots, told the county to go for him. Atkinson bowled leg-breaks, was a passable middle-order bat and chased heroically in the covers, pledging himself to let nothing past. Then arthritis got into his finger joints and he switched to seamers. The call to take charge of the side in the mid-1960s, a time for authority as well as tact, appealed to him. He liked, whatever his traits as a private person, responsibility. Under his leadership, Somerset got to the Gillette final against Kent in 1967 and were third in the championship table the previous year.

Atkinson balanced ambition with a down-to-earth streak and basic commonsense. After all, while doing the research after studying for a degree, he chose to earn some pocket-money by playing as a pro for Northumberland. He went on to reveal gifts as an administrator, notably evident when he followed RJO Meyer as headmaster of Millfield. The school flourished and handsome purpose-built facilities took the place of the dilapidated Nissen huts at Street. Buildings will long serve as memorials to his ability. The new pavilion at Taunton is another example. Before his untimely death he was seen additionally as an intuitive businessman in his role as chairman of HTV West.

Historically, administrative life has never been easy for Somerset cricket. As president he found himself involved in the 1979 controversy at Worcester, when Brian Rose's team were kicked out of the Benson and Hedges competition. Atkinson, seen himself as a future chairman of the TCCB, was embarrassed. "We did wrong but I've some sympathy for the team. People went right over the top in condemning us." Again it was difficult for him when he chaired that traumatic meeting at Shepton Mallet on the Richards-Garner-Botham issue. Part headmaster, part lawyer, part conciliator, the delicately restored dignity could be largely attributed to him. *Photo opposite.*

COLIN RICHARD MICHAEL ATKINSON Born Thornaby-on-Tees, Yorkshire, 23.7.31. RHB, LBG/RM. Cap 1961. Captain 1965-67. SFC: 163 matches; 3772 runs @ 19.05; HS 97 v Warwickshire, Edgbaston, 1967; 1000 runs once; HT 1120 in 1966; 190 wickets @ 31.02; BB 7-54 v Gloucestershire, Taunton, 1962; HT 62 in 1961. GC: 12 matches; 153 runs @ 17.00; 7 wickets @ 35.14. CBE 1989. Died 25.6.91.

ABBAS ALI BAIG 1960 - 1962

Small, polite, neat as a choirboy. In his early days at Oxford, he decided he'd like some county cricket in the vacations. That 'League of Nations' tag at Taunton possibly influenced him. He wrote to Somerset and ended up accepting Bill Andrews' hospitality, though wisely resisting the bacchic temptations of home-made wine. The regret is that he played no more than 23 matches for the county — and indeed that he failed to live up to the promise he showed as a Test player, when he began with a hundred at Old Trafford in 1959 after being co-opted into the touring side. Once got a double-century at Delhi but managed only 99 for Somerset, against Gloucestershire. Those eloquent Asian wrists deserved more.

ABBAS ALI BAIG Born Hyderabad, India, 8.11.41. RHB, LB. Cap 1961. 10 Tests 1959-67. SFC: 23 matches; 1154 runs @ 30.57; HS 99 v Gloucestershire, Bristol, 1960; HT 721 in 1960; 1 wicket @ 22.00; BB 1-1 v Glamorgan, Bath, 1960. Hyderabad 1958-71; Oxford 1959-62.

Abbas Ali Baig

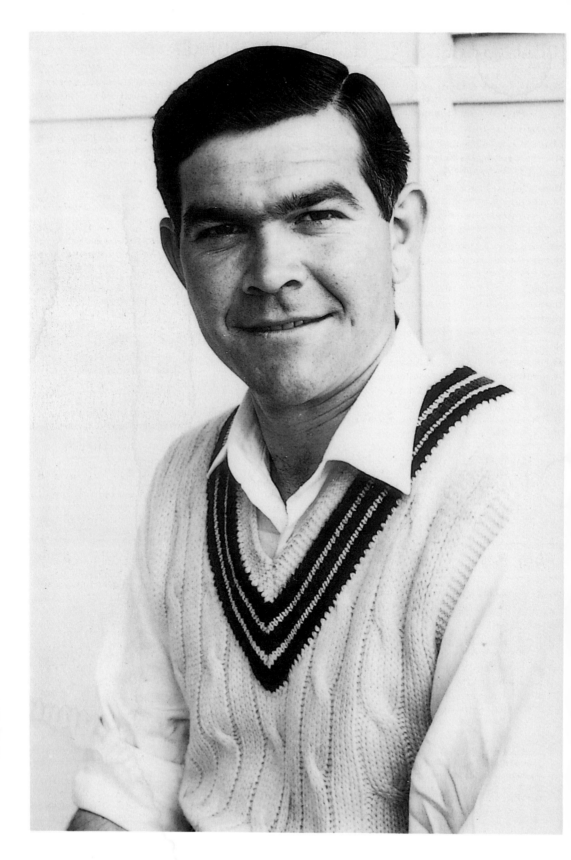

GRAHAM ATKINSON   1954 - 1966

Some felt he should have captained Somerset; most felt the terms he was finally offered, causing him to leave the county, were less than generous. He arrived in the West as a 16-year-old and when he proved he could compile 2,000 runs in a season he was being mentioned as a Test candidate. Yorkshire-born and a real pro in the Wakefield tradition, his eventual move to Lancashire could perhaps, for emotional reasons, be only a partial success. A fine on-side player, he revelled in taking on the fast bowlers at his own studious pace. Occasionally he might have scored quicker and he was not always the sharpest fielder in the side. But in retrospect one realises what a sound, maybe under-praised, player he was. He returns to Taunton reunions with genuine pleasure. Any erstwhile slight is long forgotten. We must remember that he was the youngest Somerset player to score 2,000 runs in a season. Was too much expected of him? Was someone of that natural batting talent assertive enough? Graham knew his worth and had the courage to plead his case. Looking back, it appears unfair that he left without the benefit he deserved. *Photo opposite.*

GRAHAM ATKINSON Born Lofthouse, Yorkshire, 29.3.38. RHB, OB. Cap 1958. SFC: 271 matches; 14468 runs @ 32.08; 21 centuries; HS 190 v Glamorgan, Bath, 1960; 1000 runs 9 times; HT 2035 in 1962; 4 wickets @ 59.00; BB 4-63 v Hampshire, Taunton, 1960. GC: 10 matches; 297 runs @ 29.70. Lancashire 1967-69.

PAUL BAIL   1985 - 1986

Might Somerset have persevered longer with him? County cricket is strewn with a thousand such imponderables. We won't forget his 174 in the 1986 Varsity match — or the June morning the previous summer against Warwickshire. Paul opened for Somerset and soon retired with a blow to the helmet. Felton went next ball. And then Richards took over, with his 322. Bail, content to watch, was by nature a tidy, unspectacular stroke-maker.

PAUL ANDREW CLAYTON BAIL Born Burnham-on-Sea, Somerset, 23.6.65. RHB, OB. SFC: 7 matches; 229 runs @ 22.90; HS 78* v Kent, Canterbury, 1985; 0 wickets. BHC: 8 matches; 200 runs @ 28.57; 1 wicket @ 20.00. SL: 1 match; 18 runs @ 18.00. Cambridge 1986-87.

JOHN BAKER   1952 - 1954

Just a handful of appearances over three seasons, as an amateur. Sound record in club cricket. Also played for Combined Services and Dorset.

JOHN BAKER Born Weston-super-Mare, 18.5.33. RHB, RM. SFC: 9 matches; 105 runs @ 10.50; HS 26* v Northamptonshire, Taunton, 1953; 1 wicket @ 204.00; BB 1-10 v Warwickshire, Edgbaston, 1954. Oxford 1955.

JOHN BARNWELL   1935 - 1948

He personified the 'old school', a debonair amateur who occasionally deputised as Somerset's skipper and though sounded-out didn't have the time to do it on a more permanent basis. Rightly proud of his nimbleness in the covers — and the four boundaries in a row he once audaciously took off Voce at Trent Bridge. Repton pedigree and no lack of social aplomb. Was the secretary of the ex-Somerset County Cricketers' Association when it was formed in 1982.

CHARLES JOHN PATRICK BARNWELL Born Stoke-on-Trent, Staffordshire, 23.6.14. RHB. Cap pre-war. SFC: 69 matches; 1592 runs @ 15.16; HS 83 v Hampshire, Taunton, 1939; HT 396 in 1939; 0 wickets.

MICHAEL BARNWELL   1967 - 1968

Nephew of John. Useful all-rounder at school and university level. Not a bad footballer, either, with a blue at Cambridge. His half-dozen matches for Somerset, during which he opened the innings, never quite lived up to the warm recommendations that preceded his arrival.

LIONEL MICHAEL LOWRY BARNWELL Born Crewkerne, Somerset, 12.8.43. RHB, RM. SFC: 6 matches; 144 runs @ 16.00; HS 60 v Nottinghamshire, Trent Bridge, 1967. Cambridge 1965-66; Eastern Province, South Africa, 1969-71.

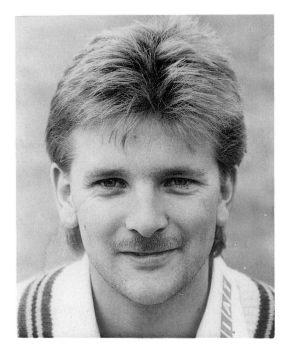

Ricky Bartlett

RICKY BARTLETT   1986 - 1992

You can't do better than start with a hundred. That was what he did at Oxford, to ensure a place in the county record books and generate premature excitement. He was cursed with a nervous temperament, though. Never able completely to shake himself free of the pre-innings tensions, was he asked to bat too high in the order? A product of Taunton School, cradle of so much cricketing talent over the generations, he was as sad as many of the locals when his Somerset career ended in 1992. He brilliantly patrolled the covers and the outfield, to underline his value in the one-day matches.

RICHARD JAMES BARTLETT Born Ash Priors, Somerset, 8.10.66. RHB, OB. SFC: 50 matches; 1797 runs @ 24.28; 2 centuries; HS 117* v Oxford, The Parks, 1986; HT 648 in 1988; 4 wickets @ 36.25; BB 1-9 v Glamorgan, Taunton, and v Yorkshire, Scarborough, both 1988. NWT: 3 matches; 147 runs @ 73.50. BHC: 13 matches; 140 runs @ 11.67. SL: 44 matches; 964 runs @ 22.42.

TERRY BARWELL   1959 - 1968

The technique and footwork were sound, especially against the slow bowlers. At 2nd XI level, with Somerset and then with Wiltshire, he revealed how well he could score runs. He was a reliable fielder and, if needed, wicketkeeper. In his county appearances, one or two harsh LBWs went against him to damage confidence. Then he turned successfully to teaching at Marlborough and Blundell's.

TERENCE IAN BARWELL Born Bloemhof, South Africa, 29.4.37. RHB, occ WK. Cap 1968. SFC: 43 matches; 1321 runs @ 19.72; HS 84* v Glamorgan, Weston-super-Mare, 1965; HT 410 in 1967; 9 dismissals (8ct, 1st). GC: 4 matches; 62 runs @ 15.50.

DAVID BEAL   1991

The Beals are a well-known sporting family in the Glastonbury area. One member, who also played in goal for the Town side, achieved local fame by regularly crashing centuries for village teams while discarding on principle anything as sophisticated as batting gloves. David was a bowler, decidedly lively by club standards and a formidable taker of wickets for Morlands CC. Somerset had him in their sights at Under-17 level and then cruelly, after being pitched straight in at the start of 1991 (with Gatting as one of his three wickets) his back went.

DAVID BEAL Born Butleigh, Somerset, 17.7.66. RHB, RM. SFC: 3 matches; 1 run at 0.50; HS 1 v Sussex, Hove, 1991; 3 wickets @ 106.67; BB 1-37 v Essex, Southend, 1991. NWT: 1 match; 0 runs; 0 wickets. BHC: 2 matches; 1 run at 1.00; 3 wickets @ 38.00. SL: 3 matches; 2 wickets @ 20.00.

Terry Barwell

LEN BEEL 1969

Was at Worcestershire, playing 2nd XI and Club and Ground matches, and followed Peter Robinson down to Taunton. Goalkeeper who played three Football League games for Shrewsbury Town and one for Birmingham City.

WILLIAM LEONARD BEEL Born: Leominster, Herefordshire, 23.8.45. RHB, RM. SL: 1 match, 1 run (no average); 0 wickets.

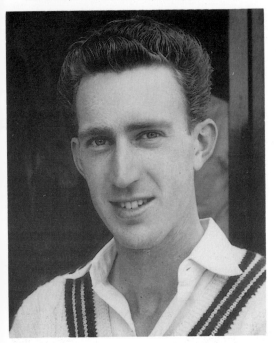

Ken Biddulph

KEN BIDDULPH 1955 - 1961

Here was a bowler often asked to keep going on a placid wicket and hot afternoon. This he did willingly. He was an Essex Man long before the social and political labels of the place. In any case, he wasn't interested in the market-place philosophy. He'd come to Somerset — and that was where he wanted to stay. For a time he was No. 2 to Lobb; his pace was well above mundane medium, and late inswing earned him a fair quota of his honestly reaped wickets. He had rather misplaced pretensions when it came to his batting. In his skilled post-playing role as a story teller he would recall Fred Trueman's words of encouragement to him as he tried to establish himself in the Somerset XI. "Don't worry, Kenny — you'll get in that bloody team for your

batting . . ." Biddulph also played for Durham, mainly for his bowling.

KENNETH DAVID BIDDULPH Born Chingford, Essex, 29.5.32. RHB, RM. Cap 1959. SFC: 91 matches; 468 runs @ 6.78; HS 41 v Essex, Southend, 1960; HT 144 in 1959; 270 wickets @ 27.62; BB 6-30 v Combined Services, Taunton, 1959; HT 83 in 1960.

RAYNER BLITZ 1986

Came partly on the recommendation of Peter Roebuck, who had seen him keeping wicket in Australia. Small and agile, with ability to get runs in 2nd XI cricket. Stayed a single season.

RAYNER JOHN BLITZ Born Watford, Hertfordshire, 25.3.68. RHB, WK. SFC: 5 matches; 33 runs @ 6.60; HS 18 v Hampshire, Bournemouth, 1986; 8 dismissals (8 ct). SL: 2 matches; 1 run @ 1.00.

Steve Booth

STEVE BOOTH 1983 - 1985

For some years Somerset searched for another slow left-arm spinner. An authentic Yorkshireman doesn't want to be taken off but Booth really was over-bowled. Not a big spinner but his flight impressed the purists. In the end, the classic case of the over-exposed slow bowler, he lost confidence and control.

STEPHEN CHARLES BOOTH Born Leeds, Yorkshire, 30.10.63. RHB, SLA. SFC: 33 matches; 202 runs @ 10.63; HS 42 v Derbyshire, Taunton, 1984; 87 wickets @ 36.31; BB 4-26 v Middlesex, Lord's, 1983; HT 38 in 1984.

IAN BOTHAM

1974 - 1986

IAN TERENCE BOTHAM Born Heswall, Cheshire, 24.11.55. RHB, RMF. Cap 1976. Captain 1984-85. 102 Tests 1977-92. 116 LOI 1977-92. SFC: 172 matches; 8686 runs @ 36.04; 16 centuries; HS 228 v Gloucestershire, Taunton, 1980; 1000 runs twice; HT 1280 in 1985; 489 wickets @ 26.52; BB 7-61 v Glamorgan, Cardiff, 1978; HT 70 in 1977. GC/NWT: 33 matches; 825 runs @ 37.50; 41 wickets @ 28.34; MoM 2. BHC: 59 matches; 1039 runs @ 25.34; 88 wickets @ 21.48; GA 6. SL: 138 matches; 3185 runs @ 30.92; 171 wickets @ 23.18. Worcestershire 1987-91; Queensland, Australia, 1987-88; Durham 1992-93.

To Somerset he brought glamour and infamy, monumental talents and unhappy headlines. He captained his country as well as his county. At his best he was inspirational, the most talked-about cricketer in the world. Bat in hand, he scored hundreds at a thrilling, muscular speed; even the mishits went for six. For the most part, he aimed straight and crisp. Then, when he snatched the ball, his outswingers were devilishly difficult to handle. Here was an exceptional man. And, the evidence increasingly suggested, a flawed one.

Away from the field of play, the tabloids shadowed him. There was often a mutual antagonism. He created some of his own problems — and his outrage against some of the papers for their prying and treatment of him lost credibility because he was himself being paid a hefty cheque by one of them. He was fined by the courts, admitted in print a dalliance with drugs and was suspended. He seemed thoroughly ill-advised in the choice of one manager/agent who decked him out in fancy clothes and claimed he could turn 'Both' into a Hollywood star.

The departure from Somerset, "in sympathy with Richards' and Garner's dismissal" has been documented *ad nauseam*. There was much needless disaffection over the years. A faction among the supporters claimed that he failed to give his best for the county. Once after a dismissal at Taunton when he was at his lowest point, he made a detour on his melancholy return to the pavilion — to offer a few explicit home truths to a carping spectator. 'Beefy' moved on to Worcestershire and then Durham. In search of an extended career, he established himself as a TV panellist; he earned a winter living from panto and popular question-and-answer stage shows based on his cricket. He acquired added charm, turning into an accomplished story teller and mimic. But he never lost a chance of informing his audiences that he could be discounted as a member of the Roebuck fan club.

His deeds are imperishable in the record books. His physical courage, whether spitting out the blood from an Andy Roberts bouncer or on one of his marvellous charity walks, is undeniable. Remember him for the matches he won on his own, the unselfish play, the 1985 sixes that went into orbit to smash Wellard's long-standing record, the frisson he created . . . the fact that he actually did savour the stillness of the riverbank. *Photo opposite.*

Dennis Breakwell

DENNIS BREAKWELL

1973 - 1983

He twitched incessantly at his moustache, pulled on his latest fag like a nervous man in a maternity waiting-room and kept up a high-octane monologue. His value to suspect morale in the dressing room could be enormous. This chirpy-sparrow player spanned the conversational gamut; from his latest catch on the River Tone to how Somerset should go after the late-order runs.

'Breaks' had three seasons with Northants before coming to Somerset. As a left-arm bowler, he was an astute container rather than spinner. He gradually tailored his style to meet the needs of modern cricket. Though his bowling became flatter as the seasons went on, the enthusiastic tuition to the schoolboys in his charge always advocated the virtues of old-fashioned spin. His perky batting was not to be discounted, even if it often had to be fashioned or sacrificed in the interests of the team. His one century, against New Zealand in 1978, was quite a revelation. "Did you see Hick's 400? Or Richards' 300? . . . Or Breakwell's 100? All at Taunton," friends would joke.

When he gave up playing, he became assistant coach at the county, with special responsibilities to the schools. Now he's coaching at King's College, Taunton.

DENNIS BREAKWELL Born Brierley Hill, Staffordshire, 2.7.48. LHB, SLA. Cap 1976. SFC: 165 matches; 3777 runs @ 21.22; 1 century; HS 100* v New Zealanders, Taunton, 1978; HT 585 in 1974; 281 wickets @ 33.23; BB 6-38 v Oxford, The Parks, 1981; HT 47 in 1979. GC/NWT: 13 matches; 87 runs @ 21.75; 5 wickets @ 49.60. BHC: 32 matches; 180 runs @ 12.00; 15 wickets @ 31.80. SL: 101 matches; 792 runs @ 14.94; 37 wickets @ 33.81. Northamptonshire 1969-72.

BEN BROCKLEHURST 1952 - 1954

From farmer to cricket magazine proprietor. And in between, he was captain of Somerset for two seasons. Each time they finished bottom — but that sort of indignity wasn't exactly a rarity in the lustre-less days of the 1950s. He was not a memorable skipper, while his own form with the bat was nondescript. But he shouldn't take too much blame for Somerset's plight. The club was in trouble financially, the rumblings of disquiet threatened at times to bring down the ceilings of the committee rooms, and the great Gimblett was at his most tormented. In the post-war years the county was going through captains at an alarming rate. If Brocklehurst, the martinet, was a failure, so were four or five others.

BENJAMIN GILBERT BROCKLEHURST Born Knapton, Norfolk, 18.2.22. RHB. Cap 1953. Captain 1953-54. SFC: 64 matches; 1671 runs @ 15.62; HS 89 v Pakistanis, Taunton, 1954; HT 802 in 1954; 1 wicket at 36.00; BB 1-3 v Warwickshire, Bath, 1954.

Ben Brocklehurst

DICKIE BROOKS 1968

One of the many who came and went in the blinking of an eye. He was signed in a hurry to take over from the enigmatic Clayton as wicketkeeper. Small and competent, he'd got a blue at Oxford and was ready to give county cricket a go. Then, after one summer, he did some serious thinking and opted for a teaching appointment at Bradfield instead. Taunton team-mates were apt, with affection, to call him 'hollow legs', an accolade apparently for his admired ability to sink a pint.

RICHARD ALAN BROOKS Born Edgeware, Middlesex, 14.6.43. RHB, WK. Cap 1968. SFC: 26 matches; 182 runs @ 10.11; HS 37 v Northamptonshire, Taunton, 1968; 53 dismissals (48 ct, 5st). Oxford 1967.

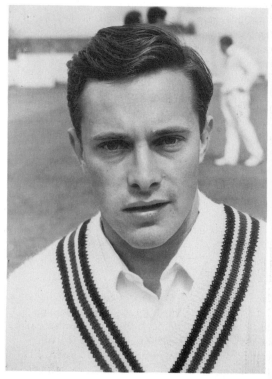

Dickie Brooks

Eric Bryant

ERIC BRYANT 1958 - 1960

There may often have been murmurs about his bowling action but no-one complained among the clubs in Weston-super-Mare and he was thrilled to be given his chance for Somerset. His first-class career lasted for just 22 matches. Against Gloucestershire at Bath in 1960 he collected his highest score (17) — and was called four times in an over. It was the end of county cricket for the left-arm spinner who had tried so hard to model himself on Tony Lock. Bryant wasn't as lucky as a previous slow bowler who had run into trouble with the more punctilious umpires. Ted Tyler, one of Somerset's Test men, survived the temporary tut-tutting and continued his career. Bryant, a brooding chain-smoker, introspectively called it a day.

LEONARD ERIC BRYANT Born Weston-super-Mare, 2.6.36. LHB, SLA. SFC: 22 matches; 133 runs @ 8.87; HS 17 v Gloucestershire, Bath, 1960; 34 wickets @ 27.74; BB 5-64 v Worcestershire, Stourbridge, 1958; HT 25 in 1958.

MICHAEL BRYANT 1982

He took the new ball with Dredge against Northants in 1982 and claimed Larkins as one of his two victims. That was the extent of his success as a first-class cricketer. They breed plenty of capable players in Cornwall and he was one of them, a quickish bowler whose feats had attracted

Somerset's attention. But he had a minor no-ball problem and never quite made the necessary transition.

MICHAEL BRYANT Born Camborne, Cornwall, 5.4.59. RHB, RFM. SFC: 2 matches; 6 runs @ 3.00; HS 6 v Essex, Chelmsford, 1982; 2 wickets @ 79.00; BB 1-29 v Northamptonshire, Northampton, 1982.

BILL BUCK 1969

Now here's a little cameo from the record books. He played once for Hampshire and once for Somerset — in the same summer. Neither match was in the championship. Both counties were keen to take a detailed look at him, as he played against the West Indies and New Zealand respectively. His sum total of success with his medium-paced seamers was two wickets.

WILLIAM DALTON BUCK Born Southampton, Hampshire, 30.9.46. RHB, RM. SFC: 1 match; 11 runs @ 5.50; HS 6 v West Indians, Taunton, 1969; 2 wickets @ 55.00; BB 2-59 same match. Hampshire 1969.

JOE BUCKLAN 1948

This left-arm fastish bowler's only appearance was at Newport. His three wickets weren't enough apparently to persuade the county to come up with a full contract.

JOSEPH EDWIN BUCKLAN Born Lingfield, Surrey, 24.9.16. LHB, LF. SFC: 1 match; 17 runs (no average); HS 17* v Glamorgan, Newport, 1948; 3 wickets @ 18.33; BB 2-35 same match.

NEIL BURNS 1987 -

He took over from Trevor Gard, and was a decidedly promising wicketkeeper whose career, because of competition, seemed to be going nowhere at Essex. Somerset had been consciously looking for a stumper who could also score runs. He quickly won his cap and, from perky middle-order, the left-hander proved his ability and occasionally pulled out a gem of an innings. The withdrawal of Brian Rose and Martin Crowe from the county scene in the late 1980s disappointed Burns. They, after all, had been the two who had the greatest influence on him when he came to Taunton. He was linked speculatively at various times with other counties and a return

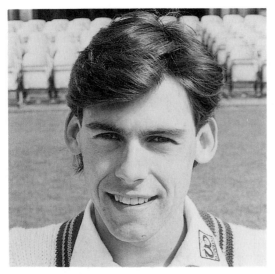

Neil Burns

was nurtured, he also played second-row for the 1st XV and took the kicks. He sampled Western League soccer as a winger, was a junior table-tennis champion and a hockey player of county potential. But cricket, for the easy-going Burgess, was the favourite sport of all. After giving up playing, he coached the boys at Monmouth and then became a first-class umpire. *Photo opposite.*

GRAHAM IEFVION BURGESS Born Glastonbury, Somerset, 5.5.43. RHB, RM. Cap 1968. SFC: 252 matches; 7129 runs @ 18.91; 2 centuries; HS 129 v Gloucestershire, Taunton, 1973; HT 866 in 1970; 474 wickets @ 28.57; BB 7-43 v Oxford, The Parks, 1975; HT 56 in 1970. GC: 27 matches; 403 runs @ 19.19; 26 wickets @ 32.96; MoM 2. BHC: 34 matches; 523 runs @ 19.37; 49 wickets @ 22.51. SL: 146 matches; 2204 runs @ 20.40; 172 wickets @ 24.62. Fc. umpire 1991-.

to Essex was mentioned. Burns was always a player of noteworthy ambition but form and, more significantly, favour, deserted him in the late summer of 1993. He lost his place and sensed that his future was in jeopardy. Other ambitions extend to business life, however. He has with his wife a flourishing PR and marketing company with sporting orientation.

NEIL DAVID BURNS Born Chelmsford, Essex, 19.9.65. LHB, WK. Cap 1987. SFC: 150 matches; 5207 runs @ 30.10; 5 centuries; HS 166 v Gloucestershire, Taunton, 1990; HT 951 in 1990; 333 dismissals (303 ct, 30 st); 0 wickets. NWT: 16 matches; 134 runs @ 14.89. BHC: 33 matches; 441 runs @ 27.56. SL: 102 matches; 1055 runs @ 18.19. Essex 1986.

GRAHAM BURGESS   1966 - 1979

It's hard to think that 'Budgie' could have played for any other county. He is authentic Somerset by birth and looks like a farmer. The voice belongs unmistakably to Glastonbury. As for the shoulders, they are broad and well made for the belting of a cricket ball. In fact, although he could hit sixes and often did advantageously in the one-day matches, he could also score rapidly with the most controlled of off drives. Like so many of the county's prized yeomen performers, he was apt to be inconsistent, selecting the wrong ball for the swipe. His bowling, off the most languid of runs, in keeping with his unflurried persona, was a valued bonus. According to wicketkeeper Derek Taylor, Burgess could swing the ball both ways. At Millfield, where his cricket

DICKIE BURROUGH   1927 - 1947

Not all amateurs, by any means, were worth their place. Burrough, the Bath solicitor, was — and he proved it with his four centuries. His father had played for Somerset before him. Dickie was an enthusiast, popular with the pros, partly because he was prepared to do his stint of chasing in the outfield. He held some fine catches in the process. As a batsman he went in anywhere from opener to mid-order. But that was Somerset. His sporadic career spanned just over 20 years.

HERBERT DICKINSON BURROUGH Born Wedmore, Somerset, 6.2.09. RHB. Cap pre-war; SFC: 171 matches; 5316 runs @ 20.93; 4 centuries; HS 135 v Northamptonshire, Kettering, 1932; 1000 runs once; HT 1007 in 1933; 0 wickets.

Dickie Burrough

BERTIE BUSE 1929 - 1953

The mannerisms were part of the fun. Preparing to bowl an over, from the moment he handed his faded cap to the umpire, it was a ritual to amuse the crowds that treated him so warmly. There was his studious contemplation, his stuttering approach, the touch of acceleration and the undisguised smile when the batsman failed to counter the late swing. The ball moved naturally away from the right-hander but he was quite capable of bringing it back the other way.

Everything about his appearance was prim and punctilious, as you would expect from someone who worked behind a ledger in a solicitor's office. The batting stance was ungainly; there was rather too much posterior, accentuated when he suddenly stretched to dab a personalised square-cut. For the most part he was obdurate. He was not by nature in a great hurry and, in any case, Somerset in those days — before and after the war — badly needed someone to shore up a teetering innings. His first match for the county was as an 18-year-old amateur. He turned pro in the late 1930s and became one of that cherished coterie of honest journeymen within the team.

Bertie, though not a swift or graceful fielder, was a useful all-round sportsman. He played full-back for Bath RFC; he excelled at table tennis and billiards. When his county cricket was over, he coached at Johannesburg and also ran a pub in Dorset, before helping out in the office of the Bath evening newspaper. Born he may have been in Bristol — but Bath, his spiritual home, was where he originally worked, enjoyed his best matches in summer and winter . . . and shuddered in despair when his benefit match was over in a day. *Photo opposite.*

HERBERT FRANCIS THOMAS BUSE Born Ashley Down, Bristol, 5.8.10. RHB, RM. Cap 1934. SFC: 304 matches; 10623 runs @ 22.70; 7 centuries; HS 132 v Northamptonshire, Kettering, 1938; 1000 runs 5 times; HT 1279 in 1948; 657 wickets @ 28.78; BB 8-41 v Derbyshire, Taunton, 1939; HT 81 in 1939. Died 23.2.92.

JOHN CAMERON 1932 - 1947

In his early days with Somerset he was known as either 'Monkey' or 'Snowball'. Both nicknames would nowadays be considered offensive. Perhaps he didn't mind but he was a much sadder and more complex figure than was generally supposed as he trundled up to the wicket and bamboozled

J H Cameron

county batsmen with his wrist-spin. In private moments, the small, stocky West Indian would confide his unhappy experiences at the wrong end of the colour bar. There was at least one period when he was desperately depressed.

He was the son of a doctor and was sent to Taunton School where he was encouraged — with a minimum of distracting coaching — to bowl leg-spinners and googlies. In 1931 he played at Lord's for The Rest against the cream of the Public Schools and in just over 19 overs took 10-49. Not only *The Times* became instantly excited. Somerset homed in on this precocious 'native' talent. He was playing for them by the age of 18.

Cameron, at his best, was brilliant. But he lost the bewildering knack. His spinning fingers got too chubby. Old sweats on the circuit, less than enchanted by the emergence of an exceptional teenage leg-spinner, gripped their handles and single-mindedly got to work on him. He took some demoralising punishment at times. There was a perceptible shift in his value to the county and two of his three hundreds were scored in 1937. In the last season before the war his career was given a timely lift when he was named as vice-captain of the touring team to this country. His last game for Somerset was in 1947 — and there was surely a poignant hint in the way he offered himself, unsuccessfully, as the county's secretary and even skipper a few years later.

JOHN HENSLEY CAMERON Born Kingston, Jamaica, 8.4.14. RHB, OB/LB. 2 Tests 1939. SFC: 48 matches; 1373 runs @ 18.55; 3 centuries; HS 113 v Sussex, Eastbourne, 1937; HT 574 in 1937; 45 wickets @ 43.67; BB 6-143 v Glamorgan, Downside, 1934; HT 17 in 1937; Cambridge 1934-37; Jamaica, West Indies, 1946-47.

ANDY CADDICK   1991 -

Off he went, during the winter of 1993, on what was for him the introductory 'A' tour of Australia. He returned with more than a good pass mark — and many sensed it could be the start of a genuine Test career. Bob Cottam had always enthused, some thought prematurely, about the bowler's exceptional promise. He had the height to bounce, the eagerness to add swing to seam, and the controlled rhythm which meant he need never take too much out of himself.

The no-nonsense action, the mannerisms, the sweatbands even, belonged to Hadlee. Caddick was flattered by the comparisons, though making a point at the same time that he had not consciously imitated his fellow New Zealander. If there had been an influence, then it was really Dennis Lillee, whose tuition had been so keenly absorbed. Caddick, a trifle dour in the Kiwi tradition, had always been a good listener. He worked conscientiously to put things right after he had gone 'just a little astray technically' during mid-season in 1992.

One parent came from Liverpool, the other from Newcastle. So the allegiance to New Zealand was never obsessive, even less so when he discovered the scant encouragement being offered him as a young cricketer. Instead he set his sights on county cricket here, with Test recognition for his parents' country as his ultimate ambition. Some at home unwisely scoffed at such notions. He came here, playing club matches first for Hampstead and later Clevedon. Despite the frustrations of a four-year qualification, he willingly chose Somerset who had shown the necessary faith in him. Middlesex had taken a cursory look at him; Surrey made it abundantly clear that they would like him. The Taunton committee may, over the generations, have got many things wrong. But when it comes to basic talent-spotting, they haven't so many rivals.

The predictable Test call came against the canny Australians in the summer of 1993. Their batsmen have a traditional relish for attempting to ruin emerging reputations. They went after Caddick and he was rapidly to discover the gulf in success-rate as he made the transition from county to international cricket. Wickets had to be earned by much sweat; at times he was made to look ordinary, something that had never remotely happened when, for instance, he annihilated Lancashire to take 9-32 in just over 11 overs, ensuring a two-day win for Somerset. So the early

Test matches were not perhaps an unqualified success. Yet Graham Gooch and the game's elder statesmen admired the temperament, the physical attributes, the resilience and self-confidence. They sensed, with instinctive optimism, that there was — with increasingly acquired technical wisdom — plenty more to come. His inclusion on the 1994 West Indies tour offered the next big test. *Photo opposite.*

ANDREW RICHARD CADDICK Born Christchurch, New Zealand, 21.11.68. RHB, RFM. Cap 1992. 4 Tests 1993. 3 LOI 1993. SFC: 33 matches; 475 runs @ 17.60; HS: 54* v Worcestershire, Weston-super-Mare, 1992; HT 261 in 1992; 133 wickets @ 24.37; BB 9-32 v Lancashire, Taunton, 1993; HT 71 in 1992. NWT: 6 matches; 8 runs @ 2.67; 15 wickets @ 14.27; MoM 1. BHC: 7 matches; 18 runs @ 9.00; 7 wickets @ 28.57. SL: 22 matches; 80 runs @ 16.00; 25 wickets @ 29.80.

BILL CAESAR   1946

It could only happen in Somerset — where, after all, the great Tom Richardson left his Bath pub to play one game for them in 1905. Bill Caesar was the surprise choice for the county the year after the war. He was an amateur, no more than military medium and of comfortable build by then. To compound the surprise of his selection, it was discovered that the 45-year-old bowler, now living in Somerset, had played once for Surrey . . . in 1922. He had three matches and took ten wickets for his second county. Between innings, he kept his team-mates engrossed with tales of his unlikely soccer career — he'd been an England amateur international, had played for Dulwich Hamlet and several league clubs including Fulham and Brentford.

WILLIAM CECIL CAESAR Born Clapham, London, 25.11.1899. RHB, RF. SFC: 3 matches; 14 runs @ 4.67; HS 7 v Leicestershire, Melton Mowbray, 1964; 10 wickets @ 21.40; BB 4-59 same match. Surrey 1922. Died 5.4.88.

CHARLIE CARTER   1968 - 1969

Opinions varied about his talents behind the stumps. No-one in the side found him anything but a most affable team-mate; and certainly the best dressed. Those who said he had a better wardrobe than catching record offered the observation with good humour. Charlie Carter was, in fact, not a bad wicketkeeper — even if not up to the exalted standard claimed by his unwavering advocate, Bill Andrews. He'd gone to

Charlie Carter

medium-paced craft. Many, including Botham, copied him. Tom hated to be thought of as just a container; he encouraged batsmen, at their peril, to go after him. He was a man of great cricketing wisdom and we can only ask ourselves why he played no more than five times for England. *Photo opposite.*

THOMAS WILLIAM CARTWRIGHT Born Coventry, Warwickshire, 22.7.35. RHB, RM. Cap 1970. 5 Tests 1964-65. SFC: 101 matches; 2422 runs @ 18.92; 1 century; HS 127 v Essex, Leyton, 1971; HT 766 in 1970; 408 wickets @ 18.87; BB 8-94 v Derbyshire, Chesterfield, 1972; 100 wickets once; HT 104 in 1971. GC: 6 matches; 42 runs @ 7.00; 4 wickets at 49.00. BHC: 18 matches; 179 runs @ 17.90; 26 wickets @ 15.31; GA 4. SL: 70 matches; 751 runs @ 15.98; 77 wickets @ 19.95. Warwickshire 1952-69; Glamorgan 1977.

Radley and then come out of the Army to try his luck at the summer game. For a time he shared a cottage with Greg Chappell, then a fledgeling pro with Somerset. Charlie was a good mixer, took the digs of old campaigners in his stride and never for a moment complained when Hampshire paceman Butch White hit him on the head. The City eventually offered a more pain-free and lucrative career.

CHARLES EDWARD PEERS CARTER Born Richmond, Surrey, 7.8.47. RHB, WK. SFC: 26 matches; 73 runs @ 2.92; HS 16 v Middlesex, Lord's, 1969; 54 dismissals (48ct, 6 st). GC: 1 match; 0 runs. SL: 5 matches; 11 runs (no average).

TOM CARTWRIGHT   1970 - 1976

Some fuddy-duddies on the committee saw him as an argumentative Leftie. That was only partly fair. He argued, from technical strength, only when he had a personal battle of principle — and as for his radicalism, that offered a welcome second option in a game dominated by reactionary political viewpoints. He certainly had differences with people. One, when he was asked to play at a time he claimed vehemently he wasn't fit, led to rising passions and his unscheduled departure from the club. He'd been suspended in the process. But he also had many admirers, those who rated a man who stuck to his guns and possessed an independent spirit. He came from Warwickshire, for whom he'd once hit a double-century, and ended up with Glamorgan. At Somerset he was soon topping the bowling with that unequalled

BOB CLAPP   1972 - 1977

Brian Close used to call him 'Bob Flap' because he claimed that Clapp always looked rather tense. He earned marks for endeavour as befits a future schoolmaster — as he was then. His forte was the Sunday League and his name went into the record books for the most wickets in a season.

ROBERT JOHN CLAPP Born Weston-super-Mare, 12.12.48. RHB, RM. SFC: 15 matches; 49 runs @ 4.45; HS 32 v Lancashire, Old Trafford, 1975; 25 wickets @ 29.36; BB 3-15 v Northamptonshire, Northampton, 1975; HT 8 in 1975. GC: 4 matches; 1 run at 1.00; 6 wickets @ 20.33. BHC: 12 matches; 7 runs @ 1.75; 18 wickets @ 22.61. SL: 23 matches; 16 runs @ 8.00; 52 wickets @ 13.92.

Bob Clapp

Fred Castle

GREG CHAPPELL 1968 - 1969

What else is there to write about Australia's richly talented captain? These were exploratory days with Somerset, where he came as a 19-year-old to work out for himself the vagaries of our green seamers' wickets and, in just two years, to broaden his cricketing education at the most pragmatic of universities. If Somerset seemingly took a chance in bringing this slim, unknown lad over, he rewarded them with some astonishingly mature skills. Those who watched him at work admired his dedication and the rapidity with which he learned to avoid the pitfalls. Graham Burgess used to say: "When Greg goes out to bat, he reminds me of a captain in the Guards."
He scored the first hundred in the Sunday League (captured on TV), at times batted as though he'd been around for years and gave up spinners himself for balls that moved through the air. His influence rubbed off on others. Somerset would have like him to hang around longer.
Photo opposite.

GREGORY STEPHEN CHAPPELL Born Adelaide, South Australia, 7.8.48. RHB, RM/LB. Cap 1968. 87 Tests 1970-83. 74 LOI 1971-83. SFC: 52 matches; 2493 runs @ 30.04; 3 centuries; HS 148 v Middlesex, Weston-super-Mare, 1968; 1000 runs twice; HT 1330 in 1969; 71 wickets @ 27.70; BB 7-40 v Yorkshire, Headingley, 1969; HT 45 in 1969. GC: 2 matches; 20 runs @ 10.00; 1 wicket @ 33.00. SL: 15 matches; 456 runs @ 38.00; 22 wickets @ 17.77. South Australia 1966-73; Queensland, Australia, 1973-84.

FRED CASTLE 1946 - 1949

If he hadn't been a headmaster in Bath, he could easily have ended up a professional cricketer with Somerset (or his native Kent, who had already sounded him out). Or maybe a professional footballer with Crystal Palace. That's only half of it. He was a fine conjurer and a thoroughly passable baritone in Gilbert and Sullivan. But sport was probably his favourite hobby; he was a natural at most ball games, representing both Kent and Somerset at hockey.

His high-scoring consistency in club cricket at Bath brought him the inevitable invitation to play for Somerset. It was never easy getting time off. He'd spend a few hours at school in the morning and then, for Bath matches, chase to the Recreation Ground in time for the first over. The holiday fixtures were far less complicated. Fred was a stylish bat who never quite found his best form during intermittent appearances for the county. But his pupils, on the boundary, treated him as a hero.

FREDERICK CASTLE Born Elham, Kent, 9.4.09. RHB. Cap 1946. SFC: 23 matches; 686 runs @ 20.79; HS 60* v Surrey, Weston-super-Mare, 1946; HT 311 in 1946; 1 wicket @ 43.00; BB 1-16 v Cambridge U, Bath, 1946.

BORIS COLLINGWOOD 1953

Once only: at Clarence Park. The middle-order bat came on the strength of his Cambridge blue and reputation on the field.

BORIS ESMOND COLLINGWOOD Born Lewisham, London, 8.1.20. RHB. SFC: 1 match; 16 runs @ 8.00. HS 15 v Nottinghamshire, Weston-super-Mare, 1953. Cambridge U 1948. Died 18.11.68.

Tony Clarkson

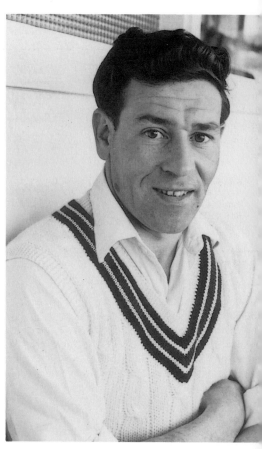

Geoff Clayton

TONY CLARKSON   1966 - 1971

Somerset and Gloucestershire fought over him
when he came down from his native Yorkshire to
pursue an engineering career with Bath City
Council. He'd had a few matches for Yorkshire.
Now with Somerset he integrated easily and at
times opened the innings with some resolve. He
was able to show a straight bat or chase a Sunday
League century. Later it was back to the leagues
and with the local clubs he used to know so well.
Nowadays he's an architectural and civil
engineering design consultant (a title almost as
long as one of his worthy innings) and, after more
than 20 years, may be close to returning to
first-class cricket as an umpire.

ANTHONY CLARKSON Born Killinghall, Yorkshire, 5.9.39. RHB,
OB. Cap 1968. SFC: 104 matches; 4378 runs @ 25.75; 2 centuries;
HS 131 v Northamptonshire, Northampton, 1969; 1000 runs twice;
HT 1246 in 1970; 8 wickets @ 34.38; BB 3-51 v Essex, Yeovil, 1967.
GC: 8 matches; 166 runs @ 20.75; 0 wickets. SL: 42 matches; 596
runs @ 16.11; 2 wickets @ 28.00. Yorkshire 1963.

GEOFF CLAYTON   1965 - 1967

There is a case to be made out that here was,
technically, one of the best wicketkeepers the
county ever had, a canny replacement for the
talented Stephenson. But then we come to
temperament. 'Chimp' had left Lancashire in not
the most cordial of circumstances. At Somerset he
rarely courted popularity and certainly
antagonised some by the cussed individuality of
his personality. He was never one to kowtow;
team-mates and observers detected the chip that
was reluctant to leave his shoulder. He was, in the
modern idiom, his own man. Colin Atkinson
claimed he was once so annoyed by Clayton's
go-slow attitude in a match that he threatened to
send him off. In spite of all that, he was as all the
players readily acknowledged, a fine wicketkeeper

GEOFFREY CLAYTON Born Mossley, Lancashire, 3.2.38. RHB,
WK. Cap 1965. SFC: 89 matches; 1744 runs @ 14.78; 1 century; HS
106 v Middlesex, Taunton, 1965; HT 620 in 1966; 242 dismissals (209
ct, 33 st). GC: 12 matches; 87 runs @ 12.43. Lancashire 1959-64.

JACK CONIBERE   1950

In the Wiveliscombe area his sporting reputation
was assured. As a club cricketer, his left-arm pace
brought plenty of wickets. He savoured his one
first-class visit to Edgbaston and came away with
four honest wickets. He was probably a better
rugby player, representing his county with typical
zeal.

WILLIAM JACK CONIBERE Born Wiveliscombe, Somerset,
11.8.23. RHB, LMF. SFC: 4 matches; 16 runs @ 3.20; HS 8 v
Hampshire, Bournemouth, 1950; 7 wickets @ 31.43; BB 4-66 v
Warwickshire, Edgbaston, 1950. Died 19.8.82.

MATTHEW CLEAL   1988 - 1991

Authentic Yeovil, so he was to be seen inevitably,
foolishly, as Botham's understudy. Had his
moment of deserved glory, with four wickets
against the West Indians. But the likeable,
easy-going Matthew, who showed a valued
aptitude in helping schoolboy players, was never
going to be quite fast enough. And injury was to
frustrate his aspirations.

MATTHEW WILLIAM CLEAL Born Yeovil, 23.7.69. RHB, RMF. SFC:
15 matches; 165 runs @ 9.17; HS 30 v Leicestershire, Taunton, 1989;
26 wickets @ 34.96; BB: 4-41 v West Indians, Taunton, 1988 (debut);
HT 20 in 1988. NWT: 2 matches; 28 runs at 28.00; 2 wickets @ 43.00.
BHC: 2 matches, 18 runs @ 18.00; 0 wickets. SL: 13 matches; 57
runs @ 14.25; 3 wickets @ 107.33.

Robert Coombs

ROBERT COOMBS   1985 - 1986

On the evidence of a wet Weston wicket, where he
took five impressive scalps against Middlesex on
his debut, some local pundits were convinced that
here was the left-arm spinner the county had
consistently searched for. He was a student at
Exeter and had played for Dorset and Hants. But
enthusiasm for him lessened and his career lasted
for an unlucky 13 matches.

ROBERT VINCENT JEROME COOMBS Born Barnet, Hertfordshire,
20.7.59. RHB, SLA. SFC: 13 matches; 32 runs @ 5.33; HS 18 v
Gloucestershire, Bristol, 1986; 32 wickets @ 34.75; BB 5-58 v
Middlesex, Weston-super-Mare, 1985 (debut).

GEOF COURTENAY   1947

This former Sherborne School boy made his
debut at Taunton. Somerset were in trouble and
he, at No. 5, soon found himself partnering
Gimblett. His 34 that day was his best in a mere
quartet of matches for the county. He also played
for Dorset and Scotland.

GEOFREY WILLIAM LIST COURTENAY Born Castle Cary,
Somerset, 16.12.21. RHB. SFC: 4 matches; 66 runs @ 9.43. HS 34
v Sussex, Taunton, 1947. Scotland 1955-57. Died 17.10.80.

Matthew Cleal

BRIAN CLOSE

1971 - 1977

Miles Coope

The enticing of Close to the West was seen by Bill Andrews as his greatest achievement. Yorkshire, in the internecine ways that they made a speciality, decided to fire him. Andrews read about it and immediately picked up his pen. It was an instinctive reaction. Three times he wrote to Close, without getting a reply. Then, with a phone call or two and invitation to stay a few days to talk things over, the move was clinched. From the steel of Headingley to the supposedly soft-bellied aura of Taunton. It was a culture shock all round. Committee members, who had initially been lukewarm to the proposed arrival of the Yorkshire maverick, could soon see signs of change. Some of the younger pros quaked as he shook them from their natural lethargy in the field. He stationed himself at short-leg, of course, and led by example. There were five centuries in his first summer with Somerset, one almost inevitably against Yorkshire. Before long he was taking over from Langford as skipper. He was full of contradictions; he'd berate a slumbering team-mate before putting his arm round the youngster's shoulders and saying: "Don't worry, lad, I'm really a sentimental old sod." He would lead with gritty brilliance and then make tactical decisions that lacked logic. He hated one-day cricket, while at times excelling at it. There were some edgy moments while he was with Somerset. But everyone agreed he was a timely catalyst. *Photo opposite.*

DENNIS BRIAN CLOSE Born Rawdon, Yorkshire, 24.2.31. LHB, ROB/RM. Cap 1971. Captain 1972-77. 22 Tests 1949-76. 3 LOI 1972. SFC: 142 matches; 7567 runs @ 39.41; 13 centuries; HS 153 v Middlesex, Lord's, 1973; 1000 runs 5 times; HT 1388 in 1971; 74 wickets @ 34.95; BB 5-70 v Lancashire, Taunton, 1974; HT 29 in 1975. GC: 12 matches; 160 runs @ 14.55; 2 wickets @ 32.00; MoM 1. BHC: 23 matches; 444 runs @ 23.37; 6 wickets @ 40.00; GA 1. SL: 91 matches; 2054 runs @ 25.36; 33 wickets @ 19.27. Yorkshire 1949-70.

ANDY COTTAM

1992 - 1993

Son of Bob — and promised no favours because of it. Slow left-arm, and a ready learner. Opportunities were rare in 1993 and he was released to join Northamptonshire.

ANDREW COLIN COTTAM Born Northampton, 14.7.73. RHB, SLA. SFC: 6 matches; 43 runs @ 6.14; HS: 31 v Gloucestershire, Gloucester, 1992; 6 wickets @ 46.67; BB 1-1 v Gloucestershire, Gloucester, 1992. BHC: 1 match; 0 wickets. SL: 1 match; 0 wickets. Northamptonshire 1994-.

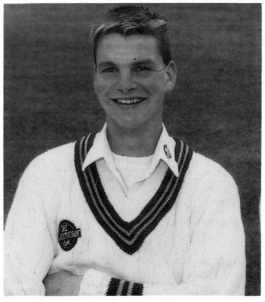

Andy Cottam

MILES COOPE

1947 - 1949

One brackets him with that other little Yorkshireman, Lawrence. Coope, despite an exquisite late cut and an adequate repertoire of shots that at times he showed a reluctance to parade, was the less talented of the two. He stayed for three seasons, leaving us with a memorable cameo or two. Lack of consistency was his undoing.

MILES COOPE Born Gildersome, Yorkshire, 28.11.16. RHB, LB. Cap 1947. SFC: 70 matches; 2718 runs @ 20.91; 2 centuries; HS 113 v Middlesex, Taunton, 1947; 1000 runs once in 1948; HT 1172 in 1948; 8 wickets @ 59.88; BB 3-29 v Yorkshire, Taunton, 1948. Died 5.7.74.

JIMMY COOK 1989 - 1991

No-one recognised him when he first turned up. His was a name hardly known in this country. He was 36, had never played in a Test match because of South Africa's domestic politics, and was now Somerset's overseas cricketer. A tall, rather solemn figure, with old-fashioned standards when it came to matters of courtesy, he relished the unlikely bonus of first-class cricket afforded him in this country. Because of duties at home, it was not certain how long he would stay here. The runs kept coming — and he was with Somerset for three summers. He occupied the crease with a minimum of movement; there was no extrovert flourish in his stroke-making. His placement was his forte, so he maintained a decent pace with twos and threes. The boundaries, often effortless, were dignified calculations — they were seldom struck. His triple-century at Sophia Gardens was a perfectly controlled entity, almost unmemorable in terms of dynamics. Jimmy pulled on his moustache between overs, allowing himself no other outward emotion. There was a serenity among the temperament. When at last it was South Africa's turn to be recognised again, he was virtually overlooked. The rebuff must have hurt. Somerset persuaded some richly gifted overseas players to join them; he is there with the best. *Photo opposite.*

STEPHEN JAMES COOK Born Johannesburg, South Africa, 31.7.53. RHB. Cap 1989. 3 Tests 1992-. 4 LOI 1991-. SFC: 71 matches; 7604 runs @ 72.42; 28 centuries; HS 313* v Glamorgan, Cardiff, 1990; 2000 runs 3 times; HT 2755 in 1991; 2 wickets @ 34.00; BB 2-25 v Derbyshire, Taunton, 1990. NWT: 7 matches; 177 runs @ 25.28. BHC: 16 matches; 854 runs @ 53.37; GA 2. SL: 47 matches; 2004 runs @ 46.60. Transvaal, South Africa, 1972-.

RICHARD COOPER 1972

Here was the Colin Milburn of the West Country, at least in build and vigorous talent at the crease. He was fashioned for one-day cricket and, for a roly-poly man, was no slouch in the field or when chasing for singles. Once scored a hundred in each innings for his native Wilts against Somerset II, and that led to overtures. Few club players made more runs at his lively pace. An enigmatic figure, who was never going to conform easily to the disciplines of county cricket, he was proud of his one gold award and disappointed that he made only one championship appearance. He played for Wiltshire from 1969 till the time of his death, aged 44, within days of his hero, Milburn, from a similar heart attack.

RICHARD CLAUDE COOPER Born Malmesbury, Wiltshire, 9.12.45. RHB. SFC: 1 match; 4 runs @ 2.00; HS 4 v Nottinghamshire, Trent Bridge, 1972. BHC: 3 matches; 188 runs @ 62.67; 0 wickets; GA 1. SL: 10 matches; 155 runs @ 17.22. Died 14.3.90.

DAVID COX 1969

One match, at the United Services ground, Portsmouth, and one wicket — thanks to Brian Rose's catch in the gully.

DAVID WILLIAM COX Born Oakhill, Somerset, 19.5.46. RHB, RFM. SFC: 1 match; 8 runs @ 4.00; HS 8 v Hampshire, Portsmouth, 1969; 1 wicket @ 77.00; BB 1-50 same match.

Richard Cooper

MARTIN CROWE 1984 - 1988

His arrival as an unknown 21-year-old, to deputise while Richards and Garner were otherwise engaged, was a revelation. After a tentative start as he got used to greenish conditions — and seemed a trifle sensitive to kindly criticism — he showed everyone his worth. It was considerable. He scored nearly 2,000 runs, invariably building his innings with all the proficiency of an experienced architect who aimed for handsome, aesthetic standards. The stroke-play was clean; the technique that of an infinitely older batsman. Off the field he was a thoroughly serious young man, full of enthusiasm for the game, strong on etiquette and good behaviour. He encouraged some of the county's promising fledgelings to meet with him and talk — about cricket. It was something new. Here, observers were beginning to say, was Somerset's next captain. They also compared him favourably with Richards. That was silly — and mischievous. In any case, the two were outstanding, and very different. And, because of the overseas rule, those theories about Crowe's ability to lead the county were simply not based on practicality. When he did return to Somerset, everyone noticed he was a changed man; tougher in his ways, shorn a little of that endearing earlier innocence. He was still a fine, classical batsman but eventually illness and back trouble caused him to return to New Zealand. *Photo opposite.*

MARTIN DAVID CROWE Born Auckland, New Zealand, 22.9.62. RHB, RMF. Cap 1984. 66 Tests 1982-. 133 LOI 1982-. SFC: 48 matches; 3984 runs @ 59.46; 14 centuries; HS 206* v Warwickshire, Edgbaston, 1987; 1000 runs twice; HT 1870 in 1984; 44 wickets @ 33.02; BB 5-66 v Leicestershire, Grace Road, 1984; HT 44 in 1984. NWT: 4 matches; 143 runs @ 35.75; 6 wickets @ 12.50; MoM 1. BHC 10 matches; 393 runs @ 49.12; 15 wickets @ 24.53; GA 3. SL: 28 matches; 841 runs @ 31.14; 10 wickets @ 42.60. Auckland, New Zealand, 1979-83; Central Districts, New Zealand, 1983-.

JOHN CURRIE 1953

Remembered more for his rugby, of course. The big Clifton and Bristol forward played 25 times for England, a formidable adversary in the line-outs because of his height and build. As a cricketer, he was a batsman with powerful shoulders; a blue eluded him at Oxford. And he wasn't around long enough at the crease, on his solitary game for Somerset, to make much of a mark at Bath.

JOHN DAVID CURRIE Born Clifton, Bristol, 3.5.32. RHB. SFC: 1 match; 17 runs @ 8.50; HS 13 v Leicestershire, Bath, 1953. Oxford 1956-57. Died 8.12.90.

CLIVE DAVEY 1953 - 1955

Solid record as a club cricketer led to 13 games for Somerset in the mid-1950s.

CLIVE FREDERICK DAVEY Born North Petherton, Somerset, 2.6.32. RHB. SFC: 13 matches; 261 runs @ 12.43; HS 46 v Leicestershire, Bath, 1955.

MARK DAVIS 1982 - 1987

High on the list of the county's 'nearly men'. Off that modest run, the pace could be deceptive — and so could the movement. The village of Kilve, generously represented by the Davis family on the local cricket pitch, was proud of Mark's undoubted promise. He would slant the ball awkwardly across the batsman, while the slips picked up the catches. At his best, briefly alas, his name was being mentioned in the more elevated reaches of the game. Injuries worked against him and his county career sadly tailed away. After that, he played some league cricket in Wales. "One of my big disappointments," coach Peter Robinson used to say.

MARK RICHARD DAVIS Born Kilve, Somerset, 26.2.62. LHB, LFM. SFC: 77 matches; 803 runs @ 14.60; HS 60* v Glamorgan, Taunton, 1984; HT 315 in 1985; 149 wickets @ 35.62; BB 7-55 v Northamptonshire, Northampton, 1984; HT 66 in 1984. NWT: 4 matches; 6 runs @ 6.00; 2 wickets @ 66.00. BHC: 14 matches; 74 runs @ 8.22; 16 wickets @ 30.56; GA 1. SL: 39 matches; 54 runs @ 7.71; 29 wickets @ 36.06.

Mark Davis

Ken Day

KEN DAY 1950 - 1956

Bristol club cricket had few better wicketkeepers. He was also a Somerset lad and it seemed logical, when Stephenson was unfit, for Day to take over. He did it seven times; his trusted reflexes accounted for eight stumpings. In different circumstances he could well have established himself at county level. As a batsman he took few risks, scoring more than 30 centuries for Knowle CC as a reward for that diligence.

FREDERICK GORDON KENNETH DAY Born Yatton, Somerset, 25.6.19. RHB, WK. SFC: 7 matches; 201 runs @ 18.27; HS 56* v Lancashire, Old Trafford, 1956; 15 dismissals (7ct, 8st). Died 9.12.91.

PETER DENNING 1969 - 1984

Dasher' he was — in the way he hurtled for singles, wearing pads that usually looked too big for him. As a left-handed batsman, he made no claims as a stylist. He was proud of his Chewton carve (reasonably enough for a butcher's son) and admitted that he always gave gully a fair chance of success. He was modest about the achievements that punctuated his wholehearted career, embarrassed by compliments and ever

ready to disparage his talents. In fact, he was a fine team-mate, unselfish in the way he batted and only critical of those he felt didn't try hard enough. The gently rebellious streak in him was demonstrated in his contempt for the wardrobe and the length of his flaxen hair. He was quite a paradox; he was gruffly amusing, one of the village lads. And yet he rode with the Mendip Hunt a few times and was captain of cricket at Millfield, where Colin Atkinson detected the strong tactical sense in him. Hidden beneath all that self-mockery were some memorable innings, both ferocious and fighting. He's there in the record books for his 310-run stand for the fourth wicket with Ian Botham ("I leaned on my bat and let him get on with it", 'Dasher' would say, failing to mention that he still scored 98). He frequently opened the innings, was an exciting natural for the one-day matches and patrolled the covers with flawless vigilance. *Photo opposite.*

PETER WILLIAM DENNING Born Chewton Mendip, Somerset, 16.12.49. LHB, ROB. Cap 1973. SFC: 269 matches; 11559 runs @ 28.68; 8 centuries; HS 184 v Nottinghamshire, Trent Bridge, 1980; 1000 runs 6 times; HT 1222 in 1979; 1 wicket @ 96.00; BB 1-4 v Derbyshire, Derby, 1974. GC/NWT: 31 matches; 888 runs @ 32.89; 0 wickets; MoM 4. BHC: 58 matches; 1339 runs @ 27.33; 0 wickets; GA 3. SL: 191 matches; 4565 runs @ 27.50; 0 wickets.

DAVID DESHON 1947 - 1953

Something of a schoolboy star at Sherborne. He seldom seemed to fail as a forceful batsman and once scored a hundred before lunch in a wartime public schools' representative match at Lord's. He was to become a major in the Army, captaining the Service at cricket. He collapsed and died at Heathrow airport.

DAVID PETER TOWER DESHON Born London, 19.6.23. RHB. SFC: 4 matches; 82 runs @ 11.71; HS 21 v Middlesex, Taunton, 1947. Died 18.1.92.

WILLIAM DEAN 1952

This Yorkshireman came down for a trial on the recommendation of Johnny Lawrence. He made a circumspect 21 against the Indians in 1952 — and that was it. The North Country proved quite a nursery in those barren days.

WILLIAM HENRY DEAN Born Leeds, Yorkshire, 25.11.28. RHB, RFM. SFC: 1 match; 21 runs @ 21.00; HS 21 v Indians, Taunton, 1952; 0 wickets.

David Doughty

ball, with typical resolve and visible pride. His merits were more often evident as the reliable back-up man. Frome never produced a better workhorse. That was where he used to play, along with his numerous brothers. Once he somehow held onto a fierce return catch from a young Lansdown adventurer, out first ball. Viv Richards was the batsman. "Who's this beanpole?" he asked afterwards in admiration. 'Herbie' was true Somerset, authentic as the Mendips. He never imagined he'd make it as a cricket pro. He was first an apprentice toolmaker and eventually returned to engineering. Bristol City nearly took him on as centre-forward. He settled for the likes of Frome Town, Welton Rovers and Odd Down instead. *Photo opposite.*

COLIN HERBERT DREDGE Born Frome, Somerset, 4.8.54. LHB, RMF. Cap 1978. SFC: 194 matches; 2182 runs @ 13.99; HS 56* v Yorkshire, Harrogate, 1977; HT 317 in 1982; 443 wickets @ 30.11; BB 6-37 v Gloucestershire, Bristol, 1981; HT 63 in 1980. GC/NWT: 26 matches; 28 runs @ 5.60; 39 wickets @ 22.26; MoM 1. BHC: 42 matches; 99 runs at 9.90; 60 wickets @ 23.18. SL: 141 matches; 337 runs @ 11.62; 154 wickets @ 27.10.

DAVID DOUGHTY 1963 - 1964

He could never make up his mind whether he wanted to be a professional cricketer or a TV dramatist. His writing was done in the early hours of the morning, as he tried to land his first play. In those days, George Orwell was his literary idol. But there was also his cricket, of course. At Alf Gover's School he met Arthur Wellard and discussed a possible move to Somerset. There had already been links with several other counties, including Surrey, Leicestershire and Essex. He had one marvellous match, with 11 wickets, against Derbyshire at Weston. Length and some confidence drifted away after that.

DAVID GEORGE DOUGHTY Born Chiswick, London, 9.11.37. LHB, SLA. SFC: 17 matches; 104 runs @ 6.93; HS 22 v Australians, Taunton, 1964; 35 wickets @ 20.29; BB 6-58 v Derbyshire, Weston-super-Mare, 1963; HT 35 in 1963. GC: 1 match; 20 runs @ 20.00; 1 wicket @ 31.00.

COLIN DREDGE 1976 - 1988

The bowling action was inclined to send coaches into apoplexy. But any apparent lack of co-ordination was offset by the size of his Somerset heart. On occasions he took the new

TOM DICKINSON 1957

Born in Australia, he had a few matches for Lancashire and a few more for Somerset (a reasonable mix). He was a useful bowler, well above medium-pace. As a batsman of no great distinction, he was known to switch from left-hand to right in the middle of an over. Such feats of versatility behind him, he got back to teaching.

THOMAS EASTWOOD DICKINSON Born Parramatta, Australia, 11.1.31. LHB, RFM. SFC: 5 matches; 11 runs @ 2.75; HS 7* v Yorkshire, Taunton, 1957; 17 wickets @ 18.88; BB 5-36 v Glamorgan, Weston-super-Mare, 1957. Lancashire 1950-51.

MICHAEL EARLS-DAVIS 1950

Another product of Sherborne School, popular source of Somerset amateurs. Blue at Cambridge in 1947 — and his single, unproductive appearance for the county came three years later.

MICHAEL RICHARD GRATWYCKE EARLS-DAVIS Born Hampstead, London, 21.2.21. LHB, RM. SFC: 1 match; 4 runs @ 4.00. HS 4 v Worcestershire, Worcester, 1950; 0 wickets. Cambridge 1947.

Peter Eele

NICK EVANS — 1976

This young clubman, also from Weston, had a solitary county game. Neither runs nor wickets to show for it, alas.

NICHOLAS JOHN EVANS Born Weston-super-Mare, 9.9.54. RHB, RM. SFC: 1 match; 0 runs; 0 wickets.

NIGEL FELTON — 1982 - 1988

The decision not to renew his contract surprised some. It was an emotional moment for him. Form had at times deserted him and he had never quite built on the words of enthusiasm that coincided with his arrival. Maybe his studies at Loughborough, resulting in a limited season for Somerset, worked against him. He was a diminutive, dogged batsman, capable of opening the innings. Like many players, he seemed to reveal at times a chip on the shoulder. His relationship with Kent had been disappointing — so he clobbered the Kent bowlers for 173. When it came to the sombre announcement that he was being sacked by Somerset, he wiped the tears away and showed his best form for months, with a determined hundred against Gloucestershire. They nearly took him on but he went to Northants instead.

NIGEL ALFRED FELTON Born Guildford, Surrey, 24.10.60. LHB. Cap 1986. SFC: 108 games; 4987 runs @ 28.83; 8 centuries; HS 173* v Kent, Taunton, 1983; 1000 runs twice; HT 1094 in 1987; 0 wickets. NWT: 8 matches; 303 runs @ 50.50; MoM 1. BHC: 7 matches; 64 runs @ 9.14. SL: 41 matches; 773 runs @ 23.42; 0 wickets. Northamptonshire 1988-.

PETER EELE — 1958 - 1965

Fortune was less than fair to him. He patiently stood by and on occasions deputised behind the stumps for Harold Stephenson. Then when he thought his turn had come, Clayton was brought in. Eele, a genuine local, was tidy and unshowy. His introvert nature was possibly not a helpful ally when twice he lost his place on the umpires' list. That kind of rejection earned him warm sympathy from some fellow umpires. As a left-hand bat, again without any hint of flashy tricks, he earned his one hundred.

PETER JAMES EELE Born Taunton, 27.1.35. LHB, WK. Cap 1964. SFC: 54; 612 runs @ 12.24; 1 century; HS 103* v Pakistan Eaglets, Taunton, 1963; HT 201 in 1964; 106 dismissals (87 ct, 19 st). GC: 2 matches; 10 runs @ 5.00. Fc umpire 1981-84, 1989-90.

SIMON FERGUSON — 1985

Essentially a 2nd XI player who struck the ball well. Also played club games for Staplegrove while at Taunton in 1985. Went back to good-class cricket in the London area. Once he rang coach Peter Robinson: "We've got a bowler with us you'd do well to have a look at." It turned out to be Andy Caddick.

SIMON ALEXANDER ROSS FERGUSON Born Lagos, Nigeria, 13.5.61. RHB, RM. SFC: 1 match; 8 runs @ 8.00; HS 8 v Middlesex, Weston-super-Mare, 1985.

DAVID EVANS — 1953

As an amateur — he was a chartered accountant at Weston-super-Mare — he was brought into the county side as it struggled for shape and improvement in 1953. He failed to reproduce his club form, despite one useful innings in front of his friends at Clarence Park. His emphasis on fitness ensured that he was at least as agile as any of the pros. Evans played for Wales at hockey. He died, aged 62, after a heart attack at work.

GEORGE HERBERT DAVID EVANS Born Bristol, 22.8.28. RHB, RM. SFC: 8 matches; 180 runs @ 12.86; HS 42 v Essex, Weston-super-Mare, 1953; 0 wickets. Died 20.6.91.

Nigel Felton

IAN FLETCHER   1991 -

One of the many to arrive by way of Millfield. He came in at the end of the 1991 season, responding with a well-made half-century at Southampton. But there was no follow-up for the stocky, punchy opener the following season, partly because of an ankle injury which kept him out when he might have made his bid.

There was more misfortune for him when he made his second appearance, two seasons after the first. Fresh from his exams in politics at Loughborough, he was played as an emergency opener at the Bath Festival. He scored 65 highly competent runs before being struck by a ball from Middlesex's Neil Williams, which broke his right index finger. Once more his career was interrupted, but he had done enough to convince the county that his technique was sound and he could build an innings.

IAN FLETCHER Born Sawbridgeworth, Hertfordshire, 31.8.71. RHB, RM. SFC: 7 matches; 281 runs @ 28.10; HS 65* v Middlesex, Bath, 1993. HT 223 in 1993. SL: 5 matches; 57 runs @ 11.40.

Ian Fletcher

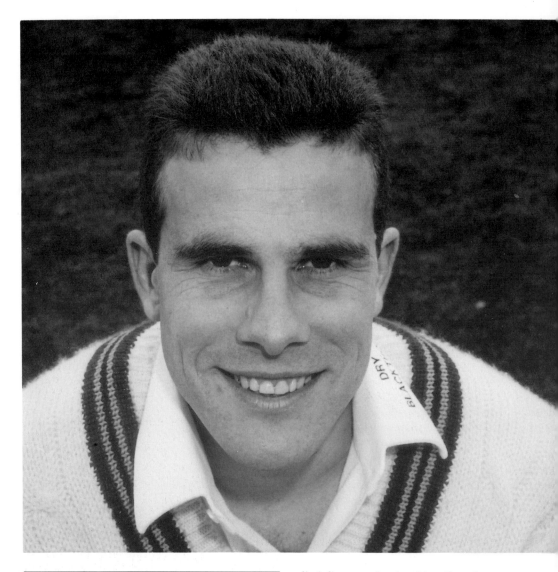

NICK FOLLAND

1992 -

How easily would he make the transition from Devon to Somerset? Had he left it late at the age of 29? And might he be, as some were wondering aloud, captaincy material at the first-class level? His pedigree as a left-hander for Devon was impressive enough. He had the footwork and the shots and was, in the 1990s, playing better that at any time in his sporting career which, team-mates had sensed, was taking on an additional competitive edge. He captained his county, Minor Counties and England amateurs in 1992, so there were obvious leadership qualities. Now that he is managing to combine his teaching commitments at Blundell's with Somerset cricket, there are new disciplines to stimulate him. Once he went to Bristol for a trial and it is probable he always hankered after a season or two of county cricket. He could turn into an exciting acquisition — with a longer playing span at Taunton that at first envisaged.

The inaugural season with Somerset brought him hundreds, several good-looking innings and progress, which if not always dramatic in the way a few had unreasonably expected, was solid. Never once did he look like a novice to the county scene — and that was the most reassuring compliment of all.

NICHOLAS ARTHUR FOLLAND Born Bristol,17.9.63. LHB, RM. SFC: 18 matches; 976 runs @ 34.86; 2 centuries; HS 108* v Sussex, Taunton, 1993; HT 872 in 1993. NWT: 4 matches; 160 runs @ 40.00. BHC: 83 runs @ 83.00. SL: 14 matches; 362 runs @ 30.17.

Daren Foster

SUNIL GAVASKAR   1980

Just a one-year contract but there were still gems to catch. One was the way he more or less bowed out with his undefeated 155 at Clarence Park. He was really only standing in for Richards, though some longed in vain that he would be back again. Gavaskar, most prodigious of all Indian batsmen, viewed his English summer with detached amusement and some reservations. He huddled in his sweaters in the recesses of the old dungeon-like pavilion and read his paperbacks between innings. He hated the cold and the rain — and wasn't too sure what to make of some of the grassy wickets. The incessant travelling, as experienced by our professionals, was hardly to his liking. But it was still a joy to have him around, if only briefly. Younger players learned from him — and the Somerset crowds felt privileged to see this stocky little figure at the wicket.

SUNIL MANOHAR GAVASKAR Born Bombay, India, 10.7.49. RHB, RM. 125 Tests 1971-87. 107 LOI 1974-87. SFC: 15 matches; 686 runs @ 34.30; 2 centuries; HS 155* v Yorkshire, Weston-super-Mare, 1980; 0 wickets. GC: 1 match; 15 runs @ 15.00. BHC: 4 matches; 225 runs @ 56.25. SL: 11 matches; 262 runs @ 26.20. Bombay 1967-87.

DAREN FOSTER   1986 - 1989

The frame was slim but he found he could take batsmen by surprise with his deceptively whippy deliveries. He was a Haringey graduate, failing to acquire that additional measure of control that would have turned him into a genuine seamer. An easy-going temperament may have lessened his progress. He hoped in vain for more scope with Somerset. At Glamorgan, his next county, he again struggled to establish himself despite the natural skills that at times came through.

DAREN JOSEPH FOSTER Born Tottenham, London, 14.3.66. RHB, RFM. SFC: 28 matches; 126 runs @ 8.40; HS 20 v Hampshire, Southampton, 1988; 49 wickets @ 45.10; BB 4-46 v Worcestershire, Worcester, 1988; HT 28 in 1988. NWT: 2 matches; 0 runs; 1 wicket @ 32.00. BHC: 7 matches; 0 runs; 6 wickets @ 43.83. SL: 18 matches; 13 runs @ 13.00; 12 wickets @ 43.58. Glamorgan 1991-.

PHILIP FUSSELL   1953 - 1956

Farming had to come first when he had the chance to extend his limited late-season with the county. As a club player for teams like Lansdown and Frome he was an all-rounder to be respected. But there were other hobbies to be enjoyed. He became a champion at clay-pigeon shoots, a skilled enthusiast at squash and salmon fishing.

PHILIP HILLIER FUSSELL Born Rode, Somerset, 12.2.31. RHB, RM. SFC: 2 matches; 10 runs @ 2.50; HS 5 v Nottinghamshire, Weston-super-Mare, 1953; 1 wicket @ 71.00; BB 1-26 same match.

Sunil Gavaskar

JIM GALLEY 1969

Jim was born at Brislington, on the outskirts of Bristol, not far from family friend Horace Hazell. He was a talented club cricketer who captained Lansdown for periods in the 1970s and 1980s. He was a stylish bat who could be both forceful and stubborn, according to the needs of the side. In the winter he played scrum-half for Bath and Somerset.

JAMES GALLEY Born Brislington, Bristol, 4.10.45. RHB. SFC: 3 matches; 27 runs @ 5.40; HS 17 v Kent, Dover, 1969. SL: 1 match; 8 runs @ 8.00.

TREVOR GARD 1976 - 1989

No mistaking him, the true Somerset countryman. He walked to the wicket, a little man with those almost comically big strides. Never without his cap; on occasions carrying the bat under his arm as if it were the 12-bore he had at home. For a long time he waited at No. 2 to Derek Taylor. When it was his turn, he did the wicketkeeper's job without a hint of fuss. There were maybe technically better stumpers in the county's long history. But he didn't often put down a catch. His two legside stumpings in the Lord's final against Kent are still talked about. Realistically, if he'd been a rather better batsman, his stay with the county might have gone on for a few more summers.

TREVOR GARD Born West Lambrook, Somerset, 2.6.57. RHB, WK. Cap 1983. SFC: 112 matches; 1389 runs @ 13.75; HS 51* v Indians, Taunton, 1979; HT 457 in 1983; 0 wickets; 217 dismissals (178 ct, 39st). NWT: 10 matches; 27 runs @ 9.99; MoM 1. BHC: 16 matches; 125 runs @ 17.85. SL: 55 matches; 88 runs @ 8.80.

JOEL GARNER 1977 - 1986

He was the most unplayable bowler in the world and when trophies eventually came to Somerset, they could usually be traced substantially to 'Big Bird'. Towering and fearsome, at times appearing faster than he was, making batsmen redundant with his lethal yorker, bouncing the ball from his massive fist as if it were a yo-yo, he could win matches on his own. And with Richards, the best and most murderous batsman in contemporary cricket, the brew in the West Country was more exciting and potent than it had ever been before.

Trevor Gard

The pair were never bosom pals as such, indeed Garner occasionally went into print quite critically about his West Indian skipper. But, along with Botham, they headed the wondrous cast in the effervescent, thrilling, twitchy golden years of Somerset cricket.

Joel liked to sleep, to prepare his Caribbean hot-pots and to withdraw from the more arduous and frantic aspects of the county game. There was something especially sad about his involvement in the *Grand Guignol* that led to Shepton Mallet. He attended the meeting, a silent, poignant figure. And when the rebels staged an affectionate farewell for the three departing stars, only Garner turned up. He had come to Somerset by way of league cricket with Littleborough; he took a wicket in his first over on his county debut against the Aussies. And he went out, by now less fit and of declining value as a three-day player, with more an anti-climax than the accord he deserved. At home, he did social work and some opinionated journalism. He would come back here to play club cricket at a tempo he now enjoyed. The West Country didn't completely lose its appeal and it seemed to make sense when Glastonbury signed him for 1993. *Photo opposite.*

JOEL GARNER Born Christchurch, Barbados, 16.12.52. RHB, RF. Cap 1979. 58 Tests 1977-87. 98 LOI 1977-87. SFC: 94 matches; 1170 runs @ 18.00; HS 90 v Gloucestershire, Bath, 1981; HT 324 in 1981; 338 wickets @ 18.11; BB 8-31 v Glamorgan, Cardiff, 1977; HT 88 in 1981. GC/NWT: 26 matches; 121 runs @ 13.45; 65 wickets @ 10.50; MoM 2. BHC: 21 matches; 70 runs @ 14.00; 40 wickets @ 13.02; GA 2. SL: 81 matches; 512 runs @ 15.05; 101 wickets @ 18.99. Barbados, West Indies, 1975-86; South Australia 1982-83.

ROY GENDERS   1949

Three counties (Derbyshire, Worcestershire and Somerset) and an amateur to boot. His county cricket was all crammed into the late 1940s.

WILLIAM ROY GENDERS Born Dore, Derbyshire, 21.1.13. RHB. SFC: 2 matches; 29 runs @ 7.25; HS 22 v Cambridge, Bath, 1949; 0 wickets. Derbyshire 1946; Worcestershire 1947-48. Died 28.9.85.

HAROLD GIMBLETT   1935 - 1954

News of his presence at the wicket cleared the market of the farmers across the road at Taunton, and the holiday-makers on the seafront at Weston. He was mesmeric — in the doting, still unsophisticated and innocent days, before the might of Richards and Botham. What was more, here was a farmer's son from Bicknoller who had hitched a lift to Frome for his unplanned debut and then scored a century in 63 minutes. First-class cricket has rarely if ever come up with a romantic schoolboy tale to rival it. He wasn't even being kept on after his trial at the county ground. Suddenly opinions were being revised. He went on to carry Somerset's batting for years and to play for his country. At his best, the style was touched with genius. The off drives could be as sweet as Hammond's. Crusty wiseacres told him not to hook; he still did so, twice in the opening over if the opportunity was there. He also liked to crash a few straight drives into the sightscreen first bounce, before the scorers had sharpened their pencils.

Harold went to a minor public school but didn't have much time for the game's establishment. He never tried to hide his simmering complexes; over the hierarchy at Lord's or a succession of Somerset officials. He could be tetchy, a man of moods and disconcerting vacillations. His team-mates admired his considerable talent and the way he so often held their innings together. But they also knew when to leave him alone with his private thoughts and torment in the corner of the dressing room. He was hounded remorselessly by depression, though the majority of the spectators who came to worship at the County Ground had no idea. The demons in his head wouldn't leave him. In time he came to hate Somerset and the game of cricket. In search of a life utterly divorced from his native county and even sporting

conversation, he moved with his wife to a mobile home in the New Forest. And there, burdened with added fears of insecurity and with acute arthritis, he took his life. *Photo opposite.*

HAROLD GIMBLETT Born Bicknoller, Somerset, 19.10.14. RHB, OB. Cap 1935. 3 Tests 1936-39. SFC: 329 matches; 21142 runs @ 36.96; 49 centuries; HS 310 v Sussex, Eastbourne, 1948; 1000 runs 12 times; HT 2134 in 1952; 41 wickets @ 50.10; BB 4-10 v Gloucestershire, Bath, 1935. Died 31.3.78.

HUGH GORE   1980

He came in 1980 as Somerset's overseas player. His fellow Antiguan, Viv Richards, who along with Joel Garner was not available for the county that season, had recommended him. He was amiable and sophisticated, though carrying, it seemed, a bit of surplus weight. As a left-arm seamer, who had played for Leeward and Combined Islands, his pace was modest medium. An injury or two punctuated his stay and he made no more than 11 first-class appearances for Somerset. He was never going to rank with the county's more inspired overseas captures.

HUGH EDMUND IVOR GORE Born St John's, Antigua, 18.6.53. RHB, LFM. SFC: 11 matches; 48 runs @ 8.00; HS 22* v Leicestershire, Taunton, 1980; 14 wickets @ 47.79; BB 5-66 v Surrey, Oval, 1980. GC: 1 match; 0 runs; 3 wickets @ 6.33. SL: 3 matches; 1 wicket @ 42.00. Leeward and Combined Islands, West Indies, 1972-79.

Hugh Gore

PETER GRAHAM 1948

One of the relatively unknown amateurs who popped up, at times at the behest of chums or school intermediaries, in the tentative years after the war. His reputation at Tonbridge had been built as a quick bowler. For the county he took seven wickets from six matches.

PETER ARTHUR ONSLOW GRAHAM Born Kurseong, India, 27.12.20. RHB, RF. SFC: 6 matches; 82 runs @ 9.11; HS: 33 v Glamorgan, Newport, 1948; 7 wickets @ 45.14; BB 3-47 same match.

DAVID GRAVENEY 1991

Already in his late thirties when he came to Somerset for a season, he'd been Gloucestershire's captain and was itching to get clear away. The move down the M5, from Bristol to Taunton — or in the opposite direction — hasn't always been a matter of approval among the spectators. They quite took to 'Grav', that towering, joint-creaking figure, as he offered helpful advice to young spinners like Harvey Trump. This elder statesman took most wickets for the county in a stay that was never going to last more than a year. His looming appointment at Durham was an open secret.

DAVID ANTHONY GRAVENEY Born Bristol, 2.1.53. RHB, SLA. Cap 1991. SFC: 21 matches; 59 runs @ 8.43; HS 17 v Glamorgan, Taunton, 1991; 55 wickets @ 39.27; BB 7-105 v Kent, Taunton, 1991. NWT: 3 matches; 3 wickets @ 30.67. BHC: 1 match; 3 runs (no average); 0 wickets. SL: 10 matches; 20 runs (no average); 11 wickets @ 23.00. Gloucestershire 1972-90; Durham 1992-.

David Graveney

CHRIS GREETHAM 1957 - 1966

'The Blond Bomber', as one or two in the team affectionately called him, could have strolled onto a film set and been mistaken for the lead. He had the looks and the presence. His appearance was usually immaculate. As one of his contemporaries said: "He could dive around in the covers all day and still not have a smudge on his flannels." Chris was indeed a superb cover point, apart from being a good-looking batsman when smoothing through the off side, and a straight, quietly nagging seamer. He would have been made for one-day cricket. Whatever the somewhat debonair image, he was a reserved, unassuming player. Once he worked as a diamond sorter, teacher and, yes, film extra. More recently he was a golf club secretary in Devon. *Photo opposite.*

CHRISTOPHER HERBERT MILLINGTON GREETHAM Born Wargrave, Berkshire, 28.8.36. RHB, RM. Cap 1962. SFC: 205 matches; 6723 runs @ 21.97; 5 centuries; HS 151* v Combined Services, Taunton, 1959; 1000 runs twice; HT 1186 in 1963; 195 wickets @ 28.35; BB 7-56 v Glamorgan, Swansea, 1962; HT 69 in 1962. GC: 10 matches; 150 runs @ 15.00; 3 wickets @ 51.33.

MIKE GROVES 1965

There was a small lobby of opinion to make him captain, after Roy Kerslake, instead of Brian Langford. He had an impressive Oxford cricket pedigree behind him,  associations with the Free Foresters and an amiable manner which bridged the remnants of the amateur-pro divide. An assertive batsman, lively medium-pacer and alert fielder.

MICHAEL GODFREY MELVIN GROVES Born Taihape, New Zealand, 14.1.43. RHB, RM. SFC: 7 matches; 305 runs @ 23.46; HS 86 v Derbyshire, Glastonbury, 1965. Western Province, South Africa, 1960-61; Oxford 1963-66.

DAVID GURR 1976 - 1979

He arrived from Oxford with a dream action. Everyone seemed to forecast Test recognition for him. He had the pace and natural movement; not, alas, the mental fibre. There were just 24  appearances for Somerset. By then, his length, line and overall confidence had gone completely. The county tried everything, including some psychoanalysis, to give him back his innate bowling gifts. He could still pitch immaculately in the nets — but it was a cruel deception. There was the time he simply couldn't will himself to play against the New Zealanders. In a hurry, Somerset were left to include two wicketkeepers, Taylor and Gard. When Greg Chappell was back in Taunton, having a net for a challenge competition, he was repeatedly beaten by Gurr. "Who is this chap?" he asked. "Is he going on tour for England?"

DAVID ROBERTS GURR Born Whitchurch, Buckinghamshire, 27.3.56. RHB, RF. SFC: 24 matches; 161 runs @ 17.89; HS 21 v Gloucestershire, Bristol, 1976; 64 wickets @ 30.48; BB 5-30 v Lancashire, Weston-super-Mare, 1976; HT 34 in 1976. GC: 2 matches; 0 runs; 1 wicket @ 32.00. BHC: 1 match; 0 wickets. SL: 8 matches; 7 runs @ 2.33; 6 wickets @ 36.50.

GEOFF HALL 1961 - 1965

Bespectacled Lancastrian who came down in the early 1960s to lend support to the attack. Once looked like a world-beater at Worksop but he lacked consistency.

GEOFFREY HAROLD HALL Born Colne, Lancashire, 1.1.41. RHB, RF. SFC: 48 matches; 90 runs @ 3.60; HS: 12* v Yorkshire, Taunton, 1962; 111 wickets @ 30.86; BB 6-60 v Nottinghamshire, Worksop, 1965; HT 46 in 1962. GC: 3 matches; 2 runs @ 2.00; 8 wickets @ 13.63.

TOM HALL 1953 - 1954

This convivial man was a wholehearted fast-medium bowler, whether with Derbyshire or Somerset. He had some fine matches and was rightly proud of claiming Len Hutton twice in a match. But as a county cricketer, this good-looking amateur ran out of opportunities. He played also for Combined Services, once for the Gents against the Players, for Norfolk and Free Foresters. But sadly we also think of the uncertain circumstances of his death. His boat-building business was doing badly — and he fell from an express train. 'Hypertension' was given as the partial cause of death.

THOMAS AUCKLAND HALL Born Darlington, County Durham, 19.8.30. RHB, RFM. Cap 1953. SFC: 23 matches; 398 runs @ 12.44; HS 69* v Northamptonshire, Taunton, 1953; HT 383 in 1953; 63 wickets @ 32.27; BB 4-77 v Nottinghamshire, Weston-super-Mare, 1953; HT 58 in 1953. Died 21.4.84.

Tom Hall

Geoff Hall

Jeremy Hallett

JEREMY HALLETT　　1990 -

His name generated early excitement. Somerset had carefully monitored his impressive schoolboy progress. They liked his temperament and competitive streak as an all-rounder. The generous prophecies gained weight when he was nominated Man of the Series on the 1989-90 Young England tour to Australia. He was one of Somerset's many graduates from Millfield; later he became captain at Durham University. Now it's a question of which career he pursues.

JEREMY CHARLES HALLETT Born Yeovil, 18.10.70. RHB, RMF. SFC: 11 matches; 35 runs @ 7.00; HS 15 v Gloucestershire, Bristol, 1991; 18 wickets @ 48.61; BB 3-154 v Worcestershire, Worcester, 1991; HT 12 in 1991. NWT: 1 match; 0 runs; 0 wickets. BHC: 2 matches; 1 wicket @ 70.00; SL: 16 matches; 34 runs @ 17.00; 13 wickets @ 38.85.

MICHAEL HANNA　　1951 - 1954

Stepped in for just a couple of games behind the stumps when Stephenson was unavailable. Tidy, adequate, and seldom made a crucial mistake, just as in his winter career as a Bath and Somerset scrum-half.

MICHAEL HANNA Born London, 6.6.26. RHB, WK. SFC: 2 matches; 5 runs @ 2.50; HS 4* v Northamptonshire, Northampton, 1954.

JON HARDY　　1986 - 1990

Perhaps basically too amiable and easy-going for the unrelenting world of county cricket. Nor did a history of illness and injury help. He started with Hants, won his cap with Somerset and then had a brief, barren year with Gloucestershire. Tall, slim and, at times, most attractive against the fast bowlers, he also ran into a few technical problems and was a repeated, occasionally unlucky, LBW victim. The left-hander remained an unfulfilled player.

JONATHAN JAMES EAN HARDY Born Nakaru, Kenya, 2.10.60. LHB. Cap 1987. SFC: 87 matches; 3675 runs @ 27.63; 1 century; HS 119 v Gloucestershire, Taunton, 1987; 1000 runs once; HT 1089 in 1987; 0 wickets. NWT: 6 matches; 189 runs @ 31.50; MoM 1. BHC: 18 matches; 490 runs @ 28.82. SL: 38 matches; 704 runs @ 22.00. Hampshire 1984-85; Western Province, South Africa, 1987-90; Gloucestershire 1991-.

on Hardy

RICHARD HARDEN
1985 -

There is always especial joy among the *aficionados* at headquarters when a genuine Somerset lad turns up. His stance didn't please every purist — nor his penchant for the sweep. But from the age of 19 his promise was evident. The exterior was inclined to be a trifle dour, though he could suddenly parade the crispest of strokes to complement the workmanlike construction of an innings. Somerset made him vice-captain as if trying him out for more elevated honours in the future. Meanwhile the high scores are growing, and the Test selectors have periodically checked his progress. *Photo opposite.*

RICHARD JOHN HARDEN Born Bridgwater, 16.8.65. RHB, SLA. Cap 1989. SFC: 165 matches; 8626 runs @ 39.39; 18 centuries; HS 187* v Nottinghamshire, Taunton, 1992; 1000 runs 5 times; HT 1460 in 1990. NWT: 15 matches; 417 runs @ 34.75; 0 wickets; MoM 1. BHC: 36 matches; 614 runs @ 19.81. SL: 113 matches; 2622 runs @ 30.14. Central Districts, New Zealand, 1987-88.

John Harris

MARK HARMAN
1986 - 1987

Maybe this capable off-spinner was unlucky to find himself competing with Vic Marks. He was a quiet young man, with a natural ability to turn the ball — and a valuable fighter with the bat. But he realistically accepted that there would be no scope with Somerset, moving on to Kent for a couple of seasons instead. In the end he decided it made more sense to opt for the profession of accountancy.

MARK DAVID HARMAN Born Aylesbury, Buckinghamshire, 30.6.64. RHB, OB. SFC: 9 matches; 121 runs @ 13.44; HS 41 v Kent, Bath, 1987; 8 wickets @ 64.75; BB 2-38 v Hampshire, Weston-super-Mare, 1987. NWT: 1 match; 0 runs; 1 wicket @ 38.00. SL: 2 matches; 2 runs @ 2.00; 0 wickets. Kent 1988-89.

JOHN HARRIS
1952 - 1959

He was such a promising 16-year-old, playing in school and club cricket around his native Taunton, that he was invited to have his first match for Somerset at that tender age. He didn't get much quicker as a bowler, nor did he grow much more. And there were only another 14 appearances over eight summers. For a few seasons after that he played Minor Counties for Suffolk and Devon. Since 1983 he has been a first class umpire.

JOHN HUMPHREY HARRIS Born Taunton, 13.2.36. LHB, RFM. SFC: 15 matches; 154 runs @ 11.00; HS 41 v Worcestershire, Taunton, 1957; 19 wickets @ 32.05; BB 3-29 v Worcestershire, Bristol, 1959; HT 12 in 1959. Fc umpire 1983-.

FRED HERTING
1960

Just seven wickets — and four of those came in one innings at Bath, where this honest left-arm seamer was surprised to find himself included.

FREDERICK JOHN HERTING Born South Ruislip, Middlesex, 25.2.40. RHB, LMF. SFC: 5 matches; 44 runs @ 8.80; HS 16 * v Lancashire, Taunton, 1960; 7 wickets @ 72.29; BB 4-85 v Gloucestershire, Bath, 1960.

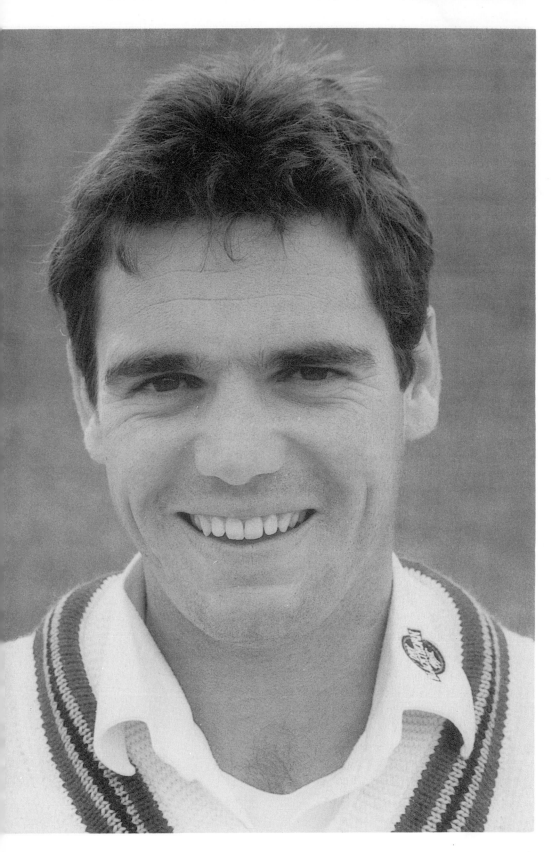

Andy Hayhurst

RICHARD HAYWARD 1985

They rushed the left-hander back from New Zealand to help prop up an injury-ravaged Somerset side in 1985. He obliged with a neat hundred against Cambridge but had only nine matches, squeezed out when the county were back to full strength. Previously 13 games for Hants.

RICHARD EDWARD HAYWARD Born Hillingdon, Middlesex, 15.2.54. LHB, LM. SFC: 9 matches; 278 runs @ 30.89; 1 century; HS 100* v Cambridge, Taunton, 1985. NWT: 1 match; 8 runs (no average). SL: 6 matches; 69 runs @ 23.00. Hampshire 1981-82; Central Districts, New Zealand, 1982-85.

ANDY HAYHURST 1990 -

When this all-rounder was signed from Lancashire, Somerset's then manager Jackie Birkenshaw confided that he saw him as a potential captain of his new county. Some have quietly lobbied for him since that. He made an early impact, doing well enough to win his cap and assure himself that his first-class career was finally taking off. Part of the trouble at Lancashire had been undue concentration on his bowling; as a result his batting suffered. With Somerset, he first filled the problem No. 3 position and also proved himself a dependable opener. Scores impressively through the off side; as a medium-paced bowler, can swing the ball away from the right hander.

Indeterminate form followed by injury worked against him in 1993. He still came back with renewed application, an unruffled approach and several big scores.

ANDREW NEIL HAYHURST Born Davyhulme, Manchester, 23.11.62. RHB, RM. Cap 1990. SFC: 78 matches; 4335 runs @ 38.71; 10 centuries; HS 172* v Gloucestershire, Bath, 1991; 1000 runs twice; HT 1559 in 1990; 40 wickets @ 61.05; BB 3-27 v Yorkshire, Middlesbrough, 1992; HT 17 in 1990. NWT: 9 matches; 324 runs @ 40.50; 10 wickets @ 18.80; MoM 1. BHC: 16 matches; 463 runs @ 35.62; 15 wickets @ 24.33; GA 2. SL: 47 matches; 897 runs @ 28.03; 31 wickets @ 30.68. Lancashire 1985-89.

ERIC HILL 1947 - 1951

He's the elder statesman of the Taunton press box, his preserve. He speaks (and writes) from experience, and with courage. The experience comes from his days with the county as an opening batsman; tall, correct and often unlucky. The courage was revealed when, with two fellow journalists, he took on a complacent and toffee-nosed county establishment in 1953. Even though the scales were weighted unfairly against the three unlikely rebels, Somerset cricket was positively shaken up. Hill became skipper of the 2nd XI; he served on the committee, and offered gentle words of help, when asked, to successive intakes of fledgeling cricketers. His affection for Somerset has never lessened. *Photo opposite.*

ERIC HILL Born Taunton, 9.7.23. RHB. Cap 1949. SFC: 72 matches; 2118 runs @ 15.92; HS 85 v Northamptonshire, Kettering, 1948; HT 731 in 1948; 1 wicket @ 55.00; BB 1-25 v Surrey, Oval, 1949.

HORACE HAZELL　　　1929 - 1952

All he wanted to do as a schoolboy was play for Gloucestershire. He used to walk the four miles from his home at Brislington, on the outskirts of Bristol, just to watch Hammond. When he was old enough for a trial, the county weren't terribly impressed. But his local club recommended him to Somerset instead. They didn't really need another slow left-arm bowler as Jack White had no intention of leaving himself out. But Horace was sent to an indoor school in London, from where the report came back: "As a bowler, he's too slow. He might make it as a batsman." His reputation was, of course, based on the precision of his bowling: so accurate, in fact, that he once bowled 105 successive deliveries against Tom Graveney & Co at Taunton without conceding a run. The post-war cricket writers noted how he kept topping the county's bowling averages. They described him as rotund and jovial. So he was. He enlivened many a mournful dressing room; he shared in the Saturday night escapades when the team were playing away. The players called him 'H'. They enthused about the way he held onto the catches in the slips and off his own bowling. They dubbed him 'The Crisis King' for the valued phlegm he could display as a No. 11 batsman. Somerset possessed some excellent left-arm slow bowlers in their history — and Hazell takes his rightful place with them. "Yet I couldn't spin the bloody ball, my fingers weren't big enough," he would say with true modesty. Somerset got rid of him a season or two before they should. How often have we heard that indictment? *Photo opposite.*

HORACE LESLIE HAZELL Born Brislington, Bristol, 30.9.09. LHB, SLA. Cap 1932. SFC: 350 matches; 2280 runs @ 8.17; HS 43 v Gloucestershire, Bristol, 1946; 957 wickets @ 23.97; BB 8-27 v Gloucestershire, Taunton, 1949; 100 wickets twice; HT 106 in 1949. Died 31.3.90.

MAURICE HILL　　　1970 - 1971

Arriving at Somerset, after a lengthy, unproductive life at Notts and a briefer one at Derbyshire, he was now into his mid-thirties and unable to add to his list of seven first-class hundreds. But his solid know-how was valued by younger players, particularly at a time when Somerset had just finished once more on the bottom of the table. He also struck the ball assertively, while setting a consistent example either in the covers or deep.

Maurice Hill

MAURICE HILL Born Scunthorpe, Lincolnshire, 14.9.35. RHB, LB. SFC: 22 matches; 732 runs @ 21.53; HS 65 v Northamptonshire, Taunton, 1970; HT 660 in 1970. GC: 1 match; 24 runs @ 24.00. SL: 13 matches; 173 runs @ 14.42. Nottinghamshire 1953-65; Derbyshire 1966-67.

TREVOR HOLMES　　　1969

Somerset's selection policy was apt, historically, to be bizarre. This Yorkshire-born wicketkeeper came in, to everyone's surprise — on the strength of a 2nd XI match at Pontypridd and typical surge of enthusiasm from the current coach, Bill Andrews — against the West Indies. He took one catch and that was it. The record books of Somerset are laden with illogical one-appearance careers.

JOHN TREVOR HOLMES Born Holmfirth, Yorkshire, 16.11.39. RHB, WK. SFC: 1 match; 8 runs @ 4.00; HS 8 v West Indians, Taunton, 1969; 1 dismissal (ct).

JOHN HOOK　　　1975

Again, one match only. He was around at the same time as the young Richards, Botham, Roebuck and Marks. In the case of the Weston off-spinner, only for a summer.

JOHN STANLEY HOOK Born Weston-super-Mare, 27.5.54. RHB, OB. SFC: 1 match; 7 runs @ 7.00; HS 4* v Oxford, The Parks, 1975; 0 wickets.

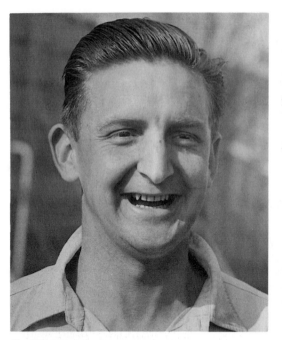

Jim Hilton

Frank Irish

JIM HILTON 1954 - 1957

Perhaps he was always in the shadow of his brother Malcolm, yet Jim served Somerset well, after two seasons with his native Lancashire. He was an extrovert North Countryman, good fun in the dressing room and useful to have around when the wicket was taking spin. At Bath, in the wake of the boyish Langford and Tattersall, he finished with 7-98 and was cheered off against Warwickshire. An uncomplicated off-break man, keeping the place open for when Langford was ready.

JIM HILTON Born Chadderton, Lancashire, 29.12.30. RHB, OB. SFC: 71 matches; 994 runs @ 10.69; HS 61* v Nottinghamshire, Taunton, 1955; HT 390 in 1955; 133 wickets @ 26.49; BB 7-98 v Warwickshire, Bath, 1954; HT 42 in 1954. Lancashire 1952-5.

FRANK IRISH 1950

He had an impressive cricketing pedigree for Devon and in club matches down there, so Somerset appeared to show enterprise in recruiting him as a pro. For his part he gambled, in the short term, by putting his business commitments 'on hold'. His early form for the county suggested that a new career might be opening up. But the runs dried up and Somerset seemed to lose interest rather too prematurely. When they dangled a contract for the following year, he said "No thanks".

ARTHUR FRANK IRISH Born Dudley, Worcestershire, 23.11.18. RHB, RMF. SFC: 16 matches; 629 runs @ 25.16; HS 76 v Glamorgan, Cardiff, 1950; 3 wickets @ 68.67; BB 2-5 v Leicestershire, Bath, 1950.

DAVID HUGHES 1955

Another single appearance. His wicketkeeping was often outstanding at club level. One of the many who made it, however fleetingly, from Taunton School to the county ground. His sole match was against Notts.

DAVID GARFIELD HUGHES Born Taunton, 21.5.34. RHB, WK. SFC: 1 match; 2 runs @ 2.00; HS 2 v Nottinghamshire, Taunton, 1955; 2 dismissals (1 ct, 1 st).

ANDREW JONES 1985

Just three matches, three runs and three wickets. He had looked a useful prospect as a seam bowler.

ANDREW PAUL JONES Born Southampton, 22.9.64. RHB, RMF. SFC: 3 matches; 3 runs @ 1.50; HS 1* v Nottinghamshire, Taunton, 1985 and v Glamorgan, Taunton, 1985; 3 wickets @ 47.33; BB 1-9 v Glamorgan, Taunton, 1985.

Who'd have thought a Turbo Diesel could return 64.2 MPG†?

The new Peugeot 306 diesel. Diesel Car responded to a road test by calling it "the smoothest, quickest diesel in its class." A car that is as responsive to drive as its petrol engined counterpart, with the ability to return superior economy. Even the insurance recommendation is a surprisingly low group 4. Choose from five, 1.9 litre models — three diesel and two turbo diesels.

†D.O.T. official fuel consumption figures. Peugeot 306 XTDT 64.2mpg at 56mph, 45.6mpg at 70mph and 37.7mpg simulated urban driving.

GLIDDON'S GARAGE

Wellington Road, Taunton, Somerset TA1 4DZ. Tel: (0823) 321321

PEUGEOT THE LION GOES FROM STRENGTH TO STRENGTH

How to put less energy into your business.

To help new and established businesses, small and large, South Western Electricity has a special service.

It's called the Business Connection.

And it's there to provide solutions to an enormous variety of energy problems.

The BUSINESS CONNECTION

Every year, experienced advisers help hundreds of companies save thousands of pounds by showing them how to use electricity more efficiently.

To take advantage of this free service, you don't have to expend much energy at all. Just contact Ken Eva at the Business Connection (0823) 335258.

MAKING ELECTRICITY WORK HARDER FOR YOU.

Keith Jennings

heart as a pace bowler. He could be moody; but gentle, too, off the field. Significantly he built up a warm relationship with the spectators at long-leg. There were some valid worries about his fitness and troublesome left knee when he came to the West Country. In fact, despite the pounding he gave his legs and back, he sustained an excellent fitness record with Somerset. The challenge to do well was just as evident on the hockey or rugby field.

ADRIAN NICHOLAS JONES Born Woking, Surrey, 22.7.61. LHB, RFM. Cap 1987. SFC: 88 matches; 530 runs @ 12.33; HS 43* v Leicestershire, Taunton, 1989; 245 wickets @ 30.72; BB 7-30 v Hampshire, Southampton, 1988; HT 71 in 1989. NWT: 7 matches; 10 runs @ 5.00; 7 wickets @ 42.00. BHC: 19 matches; 51 runs @ 10.20; 40 wickets @ 19.32; GA 2. SL: 51 matches; 116 runs @ 12.88; 69 wickets @ 25.04. Sussex 1981-86 and 1991-; Border, South Africa, 1981-82.

KEITH JENNINGS 1975 - 1981

His forte was in one-day matches. He bowled straight and economically, always a reliable container when the opposition were threatening to smash the ball around. Maybe he had too few technical wiles when it came to bowling out the opposition in the championship. Team-mates rated him as a competitor, not least for his close fielding. At heart a village boy, by trade a carpenter. Tom Cartwright was his mentor.

KEITH FRANCIS JENNINGS Born Wellington, Somerset, 5.10.53. RHB, RM. Cap 1978. SFC: 68 matches; 521 runs @ 10.63; HS 49 v West Indians, Taunton, 1976; 96 wickets @ 35.45; BB 5-18 v Sussex, Hove, 1978; HT 40 in 1978. GC: 11 matches; 9 runs @ 3.00; 12 wickets @ 28.75. BHC: 15 matches; 10 runs @ 1.67; 18 wickets @ 20.50; GA 1. SL: 62 matches; 214 runs @ 14.26; 74 wickets @ 25.06.

Adrian Jones

ADRIAN JONES 1987 - 1990

They didn't come more volatile. Usually the face was flushed and intensely competitive. Meaningful stares and oaths earned him fines as he manifested his temporary wrath at umpires like Ray Julian and Mervyn Kitchen. He started with Sussex and went back there after four years with Somerset, who failed to woo him with another lengthy contract. No-one doubted his

Allan Jones

Trevor Jones

ALLAN JONES 1970 - 1975

He's remembered for his nomadic playing career with four counties and the voluminous grunt as the ball left his grip. His 549 wickets overall were earned by honest sweat and at times exceptional pace. The successes were punctuated by tetchy exchanges with taunting spectators less than sympathetic about his fielding lapses. He turned into a calm and capable first-class umpire.

ALLAN ARTHUR JONES Born Horley, Surrey, 9.12.47. RHB, RFM. Cap 1972. SFC: 118 matches; 442 runs @ 6.05; HS 27 v Northamptonshire, Taunton, 1975; 291 wickets @ 29.06; BB 9-51 v Sussex, Hove, 1972; HT 67 in 1974. GC: 11 matches; 8 runs @ 3.67; 17 wickets @ 28.82. BHC: 18 matches; 22 runs @ 3.14; 31 wickets @ 19.09; GA 1. SL: 84 matches; 71 runs @ 3.55; 116 wickets @ 21.69. Sussex 1966-69; Middlesex 1976-79; Glamorgan 1980-81; Northern Transvaal, South Africa, 1972-73; Orange Free State, South Africa, 1976-77. Fc umpire 1985-.

TREVOR JONES 1938 - 1948

Talk of the romance of cricket and you talk of 18-year-old Jones's walk to the wicket at Leicester. Somerset were close to an innings defeat. This diffident youth, batting at No. 9, made 106, marvellously supported by Luckes. After the war, despite some brilliant innings in high-class Bristol club cricket, some of the spark had gone. At county level, that ice-cool defiance against Leicestershire was never repeated. He was still very near to becoming a full-time player. Somerset had many worse.

ARCHIBALD TREVOR MAXWELL JONES Born Wells, Somerset. 9.4.20. RHB. SFC: 21 matches; 399 runs @ 11.40; 1 century; HS 106 v Leicestershire, Leicester, 1938; HT 281 in 1938; 3 wickets @ 44.00; BB 1-3 v Glamorgan, Newport, 1939.

GEOFF KEITH 1959 - 1961

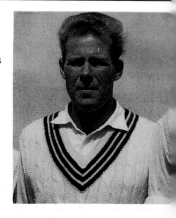

A tidy, stylish batsman who struggled for a place during his three years with the county. His one century was scored after he had returned to his native Hampshire. His untimely death came at the age of 38.

GEOFFREY LEYDON KEITH Born Winchester, Hampshire, 19.11.37. RHB, OB. SFC: 15 matches; 319 runs @ 12.76; HS 48 v Gloucestershire, Bath, 1960; HT 220 in 1960; 1 wicket @ 9.00; BB 1-9 v Cambridge, Fenner's, 1959. Hampshire 1962-67; Western Province, South Africa, 1968-69. Died 26.12.75.

Roy Kerslake

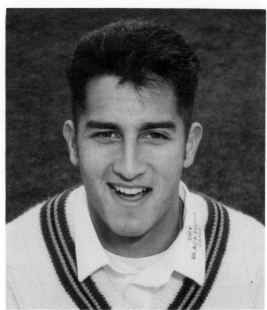

Jason Kerr

ROY KERSLAKE 1962 - 1968

His appointment as skipper in 1968 was a surprise. He was still a relative novice in terms of championship cricket; the unassuming manner even implied a lack of self-confidence. On top of that, was he a good enough player in his own right, despite the credentials? In truth he could stroke the ball powerfully for a small man, could spin it notably from the off and could field as well as anyone in the side. There was also a marked resolve beneath the gentle exterior. He still hated the committee politics, which threatened to stifle him at the time the superstars were at their most super. As chairman of the cricket committee he was accused of being too close to the players. Maybe he was occasionally, though he was above all a fair-minded, compassionate man (accident-prone, too, as the team joked when they saw him in his latest plaster cast). He probably held more secrets than most of the Richards-Garner-Botham departures and, like the good solicitor he is, kept them to himself.

ROY COSMO KERSLAKE Born Paignton, Devon, 26.12.42. RHB, OB. Cap 1968. Captain 1968. SFC: 52 matches; 946 runs @ 12.29; HS 55 v Essex, Bath, 1968; HT 525 in 1968; 45 wickets @ 24.04; BB 6-83 v Hampshire, Bournemouth, 1964; HT 39 in 1964. Cambridge 1962-64.

JASON KERR 1993 -

His first-class debut was surely one for his personal scrapbook. Brought in against the Australians, he took three wickets, including those of David Boon and century-maker Michael Slater. Kerr comes from Lancashire and dreamt in vain of a future at Old Trafford. The medium-paced seamer went on the England Under-18 tour to India and since then has worked conscientiously on improving his game as he searches for an established place in the county side at Taunton.

JASON IAN DOUGLAS KERR Born Bolton, Lancashire, 7.4.74. RHB, RM. SFC: 7 matches; 67 runs @ 8.38; HS 19* v Essex, Chelmsford, 1993; 15 wickets @ 27.00; BB 3-47 v Essex, Chelmsford, 1993. BHC: 1 match; did not bat or bowl. SL: 9 matches; 60 runs @ 12.00; 13 wickets @ 27.31.

KHAN MOHAMMAD 1951

He played 13 Tests for Pakistan, just once for Somerset in 1951 when his handsome bowling action led to misplaced hopes of an extended career with the county while he was studying at Bristol University. Three years later, he was plucked out of the Lancashire League to join the Pakistan touring team.

KHAN MOHAMMAD Born Lahore, India, 1.1.28. RHB, RFM. 13 Tests (Pakistan) 1952-58. SFC: 1 match; 10 runs @ 10.00; HS 10* v South Africans, Taunton, 1951; 5 wickets @ 20.80; BB 3-74 same match. Northern India 1946-47; Indian Universities 1947-61.

David Kitson

George Lambert

DAVID KITSON   1952 - 1954

One of the growing number that came down from the North in the 1950s. He arrived from Yorkshire with a sound pedigree but his progress with Somerset over three years, with the bat, was unspectacular. As a bowls player, he was later to earn just as much quiet acclaim and no doubt derive as much pleasure.

DAVID LEES KITSON Born Batley, Yorkshire, 13.9.25. RHB. SFC: 32 matches; 886 runs @ 15.54; HS 69 v Leicestershire, Leicester, 1953; HT 589 in 1953.

GEORGE LAMBERT   1960

It was unthinkable to some that he, a fast bowler from Gloucestershire, should have been appointed Somerset's coach in 1960. He was then 41 and played three times when Biddulph and Alley were unfit. In the late 1940s he was arguably the quickest bowler on the domestic circuit and was very near to a Test call. George was a Londoner, chirpy and very much a family man. Crowds at Bristol and Cheltenham loved him; his ebullience could restore morale in a depressed dressing room.

GEORGE ERNEST EDWARD LAMBERT Born Paddington, London, 11.5.18. RHB, RFM. SFC: 3 matches; 64 runs @ 10.67; HS 24 v Middlesex, Lord's, 1960; 3 wickets @ 53.33; BB 3-55 same match. Gloucestershire 1938-57. Died 31.10.91.

MERVYN KITCHEN   1960 - 1979

Here was the left-hander with the cheeks of a Somerset farmer and the gait which suggested that his ancestors once went to sea from Avonmouth. Crowds took to him because he was authentic Nailsea and Flax Bourton, without artifice or pretentious ambition. He was best when he attacked, driving and pulling with pugnacious power. At times early on, he must have wondered whether he'd ever establish himself in the championship team. His value to the 2nd XI had been undeniable and, scoring well over 1,000 runs for them, he was one of the outstanding successes when they won the Minor Counties' title for the first time. Upgrading wasn't automatic and occasionally his confidence seemed to be suffering as he waited for his chance. He practised assiduously — and that village boy promise was gradually fulfilled. His uncomplicated style and demeanour were much to the liking of the West Country supporters. In 1968 he hit five hundreds, though maybe he was never fashionable enough for loftier recognition. There was some surprise when he took a year's break from the game. But back he came in 1976 — and, of course, he's still prominently involved as a first-class and Test umpire. *Photo opposite.*

MERVYN JOHN KITCHEN Born Nailsea, Somerset, 1.8.40. LHB. Cap 1966. SFC: 352 matches; 15213 runs @ 26.41; 17 centuries; HS 189 v Pakistanis, Taunton, 1967; 1000 runs 7 times; HT 1730 in 1968; 2 wickets @ 54.50; BB 1-4 v Sussex, Taunton, 1969. GC: 28 matches; 815 runs @ 31.50; MoM 2. BHC: 25 matches; 504 runs @ 21.00; 1 wicket @ 8.00; GA 1. SL: 119 matches; 2069 runs @ 20.48; 4 wickets @ 22.25. Fc umpire 1982-.

George Langdale

Mike Latham

GEORGE LANGDALE   1946 - 1949

He arrived a virtual stranger, this studious looking schoolmaster in his glasses, and scored a hundred on his home debut. The jauntily struck 146 (92 in boundaries) was against Yorkshire, whose famous skipper, Brian Sellers, when asked for an unofficial reference, had joked: "He'll probably be good enough for you." On the strength of that qualified praise, Langdale went in at No. 8. The left-hander was quickly handed his cap, though the runs failed to come so easily again. This Yorkshireman had four games for Derbyshire before the war; he later played for Berkshire (once taking all ten wickets for them with his off breaks) and Norfolk.

GEORGE RICHMOND LANGDALE Born Thornaby, Yorkshire, 11.3.16. LHB, ROB. Cap 1946. SFC: 20 matches; 616 runs @ 19.87; 1 century; HS 146 v Leicestershire, Wells, 1946; HT 357 in 1946; 20 wickets @ 37.80; BB 5-30 v Warwickshire, Edgbaston, 1946. Derbyshire 1936-37.

MIKE LATHAM   1961 - 1962

One of the large number, in his case a seamer and not a spinner, to make his mark at Bath. He had a nice action and got some movement, but he stayed for only two seasons with modest returns.

MICHAEL EDWARD LATHAM Born Birmingham, 14.1.39. RHB, RFM. SFC: 18 matches; 133 runs @ 14.78; HS 21* v Hampshire, Frome, 1961; 29 wickets @ 30.62; BB 5-20 v Nottinghamshire, Bath, 1962; HT 23 in 1962.

BRIAN LANGFORD   1953 - 1974

Only Jack White and Arthur Wellard have taken more wickets for Somerset. As a fair-haired teenager, supposedly without a pair of boots of his own, Langford signalled his intent in sensational style at Bath. Aided by a capricious strip, he twisted his supple fingers ingenuously in three matches for a 26-wicket haul. Fourteen of them came against Kent. Here was a new name, an off-spinner, for the national sports pages. And was it really true that he'd been bowling acceptable little seamers until fairly recently?

He went off to do his National Service and it wasn't certain that he'd be coming back to Somerset, as he surveyed the slow bowling competition around in his absence. But he remembered the kindly words he had originally been given by Wally Luckes, who lived just down the road in Bridgwater. The return to Somerset was the prelude to a career which was to bring 'Langy' the captaincy, if not the chance to represent his country. He really did spin the ball — and his accuracy served him well. At Yeovil, when the John Player competition was still in its infancy, he bowled his eight overs without conceding a run. It's a record that can, of course, never be beaten. Once proud of his batting — at Dr Morgan's School and Bridgwater CC, for whom he opened the innings — he accepted that bowling must become his preoccupation, though he was always capable of coming up with timely late runs.

Photo opposite

Controversy didn't completely pass him by. He was, in the 1960s, one of the pay rebels who advocated a fairer structure. While he was captain, the crowd once demonstrated and turned on him at Weston in the match with Tom Graveney's Worcestershire. Later it was agreed that there was equal fault on the other side. As chairman of the cricket committee, he was awkwardly placed in the Richards-Garner rumpus. His greatest feats were to head the national bowling averages at the age of 17 and to remain for so long one of the most precise and guileful off-spinners in the country.

BRIAN ANTHONY LANGFORD Born Birmingham, 17.12.35. RHB, OB. Cap 1957. Captain 1969-71. SFC: 504 matches; 7513 runs @ 13.56; HS 68* v Sussex, Hove, 1960, and 68 v Kent, Gillingham, 1963, and 68* v Glamorgan, Taunton, 1972; HT 638 in 1962; 1390 wickets @ 24.89; BB 9-26 v Lancashire, Weston-super-Mare, 1958; 100 wickets 5 times; HT 116 in 1958. GC: 12 matches; 142 runs @ 23.67; 10 wickets @ 27.70. SL: 54 matches; 299 runs @ 10.68; 55 wickets @ 23.62.

MARK LATHWELL   1991 -

You didn't need to tell the local pundits that here was some exceptional quality. There could not have been a more self-effacing arrival. But the innate gifts were immediately apparent. He was quickly being compared with Gimblett, mainly because he, too, was an opening batsman who went for his shots. The styles varied a good deal, of course. Lathwell actually had more leg-side strokes, though because of his unassuming manner, he'd not claim to have Gimblett's sublime repertoire.

There was a thrilling inevitability about his progress from the first time he picked up a bat, this small, quite sturdy figure, at Taunton. The instincts were right, if rather less so the feet. What was more, he played the ball late like the great batsmen. No-one at Somerset was surprised when, after his first full season, he was chosen for England 'A' in Australia — not really surprised either when he came up with an innings of 175 out there.

There could be years ahead to extol his technical merits, even though we should know from experience that making long-range forecasts in the quirky humanity stakes can be asking for trouble. They may try to make him more competitive and that, for a young man with such a delightful, easy-going temperament, could rebound. At the moment he's as unruffled as a Devon cream-tea shop.

Some kind of anti-climax was bound to come, of course. The 1993 season tailed away badly, by his exhilarating standards. Full Test recognition came, with not too many signs of his burgeoning natural talents against the Australians. Technical flaws were exposed to a national television audience. The so-called experts started pontificating about his inexperience and what they claimed he was doing wrong. He did make mistakes but many of the comments were not constructive; they understandably irritated Somerset's director of cricket. Lathwell kept his thoughts to himself, though he was apt to confide to his friends that too many people had expected too much too quickly. He packed his bags for the 1993/94 'A' tour of South Africa with fingers crossed. *Photo opposite.*

MARK NICHOLAS LATHWELL Born Bletchley, Buckinghamshire, 26.12.71. RHB, RM. Cap 1992. 2 Tests 1993. SFC: 35 matches; 2056 runs @ 34.85; 3 centuries; HS 132 v Essex, Chelmsford, 1993; 1000 runs once; HT 1176 in 1992; 6 wickets @ 66.00; BB 1-9 v Gloucestershire, Gloucester, 1992. NWT: 7 matches; 270 runs @ 38.57. 1 wicket @ 23.00; MoM 1. BHC: 5 matches; 175 runs @ 43.75; 0 wickets; GA 1. SL: 28 matches; 814 runs @ 31.31; 0 wickets.

MILES LAWRENCE   1959 - 1961

Eldest son of Johnny, he gave up leg-break bowling to become a most proficient league wicketkeeper. By then his championship career, extending over three seasons for Somerset, was over. He was a capable batsman, though his father's hopes for him were clearly not going to be fulfilled. Lack of physique worked against him. Johnny and Miles shared a marked aptitude towards coaching, the son at Leeds Grammar School.

JOHN MILES LAWRENCE Born Rothwell, Yorkshire, 7.11.40. RHB, LB. SFC: 18 matches; 372 runs @ 15.50; HS 41 v Middlesex, Taunton, 1961; HT 199 in 1961; 9 wickets @ 40.33; BB 3-44 v Nottinghamshire, Taunton, 1959. Died 16.4.89.

JOHNNY LAWRENCE 1946 - 1955

He tossed his leg-breaks up into the clouds, causing merriment and consternation. He chatted as he bowled, warning the batsman that the googly was coming. But opponents and team-mates knew what a practical joker he was. His conversation, coloured by Yorkshire vowels, bubbled away — whether he was saving the game with the deadest of bats, relying on an intuitive stumping from Stephenson, "me real partner in crime" or picking up the catches at short leg. Twice he took 100 wickets in a season, once he was desperately near to the double. Little Johnny didn't approve of strong drink or strong language. His Nonconformist beliefs caused him to reject Sunday matches in his benefit year. For all that, he wasn't remotely a killjoy. His sheer enthusiasm for the game was conveyed to the hundreds of lads who attended his cricket schools in the North. *Photo opposite.*

JOHN LAWRENCE Born Carlton, Yorkshire, 29.3.14. RHB, LBG. Cap 1946. SFC: 281 matches; 9094 runs @ 20.44; 3 centuries; HS 122 v Worcestershire, Worcester, 1955; 1000 runs 3 times; HT 1128 in 1955; 791 wickets @ 24.88; BB 8-41 v Worcestershire, Worcester, 1950; 100 wickets twice; HT 115 in 1950. Died 10.12.88.

ROLAND LEFEBVRE 1990 - 1992

Should Somerset have made greater efforts to hold on to him? He could be a bonny fighter, especially suited to the one-day matches. It was unusual for the county to have a Dutchman in the side. Off the field he tended aching limbs (as a qualified physiotherapist) and manipulated the ivories (as a more than passable pianist). His tight medium-pace was not easy to score off; his batting was certainly not to be disparaged, as his century at Clarence Park proved. But 1992 was a cruel year for him, as he struggled to recover and restake his claims after a misplaced jape, in which he was the innocent victim, on tour. He became a popular and capable member of the successful Glamorgan side in 1993.

ROLAND PHILIPPE LEFEBVRE Born: Rotterdam, Holland, 7.2.63. RHB, RMF. Cap 1991. SFC: 36 matches; 650 runs @ 20.97; 1 century; HS 100 v Worcestershire, Weston-super-Mare, 1991; HT 366 in 1991; 54 wickets @ 45.41; BB 5-30 v Gloucestershire, Taunton, 1990; HT 31 in 1990. NWT: 5 matches; 34 runs @ 34.00; 15 wickets @ 10.00. BHC: 10 matches; 121 runs @ 30.25; 9 wickets @ 42.22. SL: 33 matches; 196 runs @ 11.53; 34 wickets @ 32.26. Holland 1983-90. Canterbury, New Zealand, 1990-91. Glamorgan 1993-.

Roland Lefebvre

CLEVELAND LINDO 1963

What more do you have to do to win a contract? The Jamaican had been recommended and after a decidedly whippy session in the Taunton nets, he was put straight in against the Pakistan Eaglets. Handed the second new ball, he dismissed five tourists for one run off 21 balls. His figures were 8-88. But he still didn't return.

CLEVELAND VINCENT LINDO Born St Elizabeth, Jamaica, 6.6.36. RHB, RFM. SFC: 1 match; 23 runs (no average); HS 23* v Pakistan Eaglets, Taunton 1963; 8 wickets @ 11.00; BB 8-88 same match. Nottinghamshire 1960.

FRANK LEE 1929 - 1947

Here was the ideal foil for Gimblett. The style was one of unwavering vigilance; right leg down the wicket and straight bat. He scorned the histrionics of run-making. The Somerset innings, punctuated by cavaliers and wayward technicians, needed Lee's undisturbed calm. Eight times, all the same, he scored 1,000 runs; there were 23 centuries . . . and he kept wicket in an emergency. Everything he did carried an aura of dignity. This quality was still apparent during his 29 Tests as an umpire. *Photo opposite.*

FRANK STANLEY LEE Born Marylebone, London, 24.7.05. LHB, RM. Cap 1931. SFC: 328 matches; 15243 runs @ 27.97; 23 centuries; HS 169 v Nottinghamshire, Trent Bridge, 1946; 1000 runs 8 times; HT 2019 in 1938; 23 wickets @ 32.57; BB 5-53 v Warwickshire, Taunton, 1933. Middlesex 1925. Fc umpire 1948-63. Died 30.3.82.

JEREMY LLOYDS 1979 - 1984

Some tried hard to keep him when he chose to move up the motorway to Gloucestershire. There came a time, one suspects, when he was no longer happy in the Taunton dressing room. He was an intelligent and complex person, probably feeling that at times he deserved more support and scope. As a player, he was not far short of establishing himself as a genuine all-rounder. He was good enough to open the innings for Somerset; he could punch most fluently off his pads when runs were needed. He was a prodigious off-spinner, the most reliable of slips.

JEREMY WILLIAM LLOYDS Born Penang, Malaya, 17.11.54. LHB, ROB. Cap 1982. SFC: 100 matches; 4036 runs @ 28.42; HS 132* v Northamptonshire, Northampton, 1982; 5 centuries; HT 981 in 1982; 133 wickets @ 34.84; BB 7-88 v Essex, Chelmsford, 1982; HT 46 in 1982. NWT: 7 matches; 85 runs @ 21.25; 0 wickets. BHC: 13 matches; 153 runs @ 13.91; 0 wickets. SL: 42 matches; 354 runs @ 13.61; 3 wickets @ 44.66. Gloucestershire 1985-91; Orange Free State, South Africa, 1983-88.

IAN LOMAX 1962

He was seen as a gentleman farmer who trained racehorses. But his prodigious hitting for Wiltshire was equally well-known. This towering Old Etonian went on the Surridge tour to Bermuda and the following year essayed county cricket. The experience kept outfielders busy, though lasting for just half a dozen matches. In cricketing terms, this formidable amateur belonged to an earlier era.

IAN RAYMOND LOMAX Born Fulham, London, 30.7.31. RHB, RFM. SFC: 6 matches; 267 runs @ 22.35; HS 83 v Hampshire, Taunton, 1962; 0 wickets.

Jeremy Lloyds

Bryan Lobb

Geoff Lomax

BRYAN LOBB   1955 - 1969

Warwickshire, for whom he played once, showed
no great reluctance in letting him go. They were
no doubt surprised to learn, four years later, that
he was Somerset's first fast bowler since the war to
take 100 wickets in a season. He did it by yeoman
labours, uncomplicated inswing, a bit of bounce
— and with a grin on his face. The West Country
crowds respected him for his bowling, chortled at
his eccentricities, which had more to do with his
batting and fielding. Co-ordination was a stranger
to him. He loped comically down the wicket,
unable to judge a single; he agonised and
changed direction a dozen times, like a lanky
Buster Keaton, as the ball approached him at
long leg. Away from cricket, he was seldom
without his pipe. He became a schoolmaster, with
one eye romantically on the sports field.

> BRYAN LOBB Born Birmingham, 11.1.31. RHB, RFM. Cap 1955.
> SFC: 115 matches; 624 runs @ 5.20; HS 42 v Yorkshire, Bath, 1958;
> HT 214 in 1957; 368 wickets @ 23.72; BB 7-43 v Middlesex, Lord's,
> 1958; 100 wickets once; HT 110 in 1957. Warwickshire 1953.

GEOFF LOMAX   1954 - 1962

Unruffled, unspectacular and occasionally
invaluable. Here was an artisan all-round
cricketer, who was known to open both the
batting and bowling for Somerset at Lord's. After
coming down from his native Lancashire, his
sense of endeavour and good nature made him a
popular occupant of the Taunton dressing room.
He found himself, at some time, batting in almost
every position in the order; he pegged away at just
above medium-pace, capable of his two or three
wickets. In the slips he hardly ever dropped a
catch. Geoff had one wonderful match against
Notts at Weston in 1958 when he virtually ensured
the nine-wicket win, with bat and ball, on his own.
That was where he got his only hat-trick. There
were also two centuries in his career, and hints
that he could be a perky as well as obdurate
batsman. One of his later passions was off-shore
fishing.

> JAMES GEOFFREY LOMAX Born Rochdale, Lancashire, 20.5.25.
> RHB, RFM. Cap 1954. SFC: 211 matches; 7516 runs @ 20.76; 2
> centuries; HS 104* v Sussex, Eastbourne, 1962; 1000 runs twice; HT
> 1298 in 1959; 235 wickets @ 35.03; BB 6-75 v Surrey, Oval, 1954;
> HT 50 in 1958. Lancashire 1949-53. Died 21.5.92.

'Bunty' Longrigg

Wally Luckes

'BUNTY' LONGRIGG   1925 - 1947

Back to lead Somerset again after the war, he deserved some credit for the fact that they finished fourth. In 1930 he had taken a double-hundred off Leicestershire, watched by his somewhat intimidating father, the Major, later to be county president. Bunty, a left-hander, played the spinners well and was apt to look vulnerable against the genuine pace. At short-leg, with jutting jaw and sleeked-back dark hair, he cut a patrician figure. The Bath law practice had first claims on him after the war but he was county president in the late 1960s, a difficult time.

EDMUND FALLOWFIELD LONGRIGG Born Bath, 16.4.06. LHB. Cap 1926. Captain 1938-46. SFC: 219 matches; 8329 runs @ 24.57; 10 centuries; HS 205 v Leicestershire, Taunton, 1930; 1000 runs twice; HT 1567 in 1930; 0 wickets. Died 23.7.74.

WALLY LUCKES   1924 - 1949

It may have been West Country allegiance but Hazell always used to say there wasn't a better wicketkeeper in the country. "If you'd only shouted louder, Wally, you'd have played for England." Indeed he was unobtrusive in everything he did, though the stumpings were remarkably sharp and agile for someone who was hampered by a heart condition. The constant threat of ill health caused him to bat lower in the order than his vigilant skills deserved. His one hundred came against Kent, maybe assisted a trifle in the end by the generosity of Ames and one or two bowlers. Only Stephenson claimed more victims behind the stumps for Somerset.

WALTER THOMAS LUCKES Born London, 1.1.01. RHB, WK. Cap 1927. SFC: 365 matches; 5710 runs @ 16.22; 1 century; HS 121* v Kent, Bath, 1937; HT 662 in 1947; 827 dismissals (586 ct, 241 st). Died 27.10.82.

COLIN McCOOL
1956 - 1960

When he joined Somerset, to the surprise of many, he was past 40. His influence in the following seasons was still to be considerable. Occasionally some of the younger pros didn't relish the way he treated them. Maybe they also resented that his salary was well in excess of their own. But their respect for his competitive approach and sheer experience was undeniable. His value to Somerset was primarily as a batsman. The way he played the spinners was much admired; in 1956 he was only just short of 2,000 runs. As for his leg-spinners, they could be expensive, even if used judiciously to break a partnership or 'buy' wickets. In the context of Australian cricket he was judged as a most talented all-rounder, unlucky not to be included in any of the Tests during Bradman's visit of 1948. He played some league cricket in this country and his friend and sparring partner, Bill Alley, used to say that experience ruined Colin as a slow bowler; it tempted him to push the ball down too fast. Sturdy, fair-skinned, a contemplative pipe-smoker in the corner of the dressing-room, he proved an astute investment for Somerset. His hundreds were full of wristy aplomb, and his fielding in the slips was another bonus. *Photo opposite.*

COLIN LESLIE McCOOL Born Sydney, Australia, 9.12.15. RHB, LBG. Cap 1956. 14 Tests 1946-50. SFC: 138 matches; 7913 runs @ 33.82; 12 centuries; HS 169 v Worcestershire, Stourbridge, 1958; 1000 runs 5 times; HT 1966 in 1956; 219 wickets @ 28.05; BB 8-74 v Nottinghamshire, Trent Bridge, 1958; HT 62 in 1959. New South Wales, Australia, 1939-41; Queensland, Australia, 1945-53. Died 5.4.86.

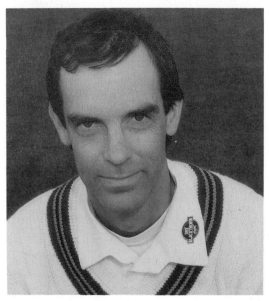

Ken MacLeay

RUSS McCOOL
1982

Born in the county town, while his father was playing for Somerset, it seemed logical — and sentimental — for Russell to try his luck. He, too, bowled leg-breaks and googlies. In the nets and 2nd XI matches, he looked impressive. Nothing much happened in his only championship appearance, and he returned to Australia.

RUSSEL JOHN McCOOL Born Taunton, 4.12.59. RHB, LB. SFC: 1 match; 19 runs @ 9.50. HS 12 v Derbyshire, Derby, 1982; 0 wickets.

KEN MacLEAY
1991 - 1992

It looked like quite a coup when it was first announced that he was coming over from Australia, for whom he'd played in 16 one-day internationals, to join Somerset. He had been born at Bradford-on-Avon, while his father was in the Navy here, and although the family soon emigrated, it was the perfect cricketing qualification. Vic Marks, who had seen him in action for Western Australia, added his recommendations. But bowling successes were relatively elusive and he often seemed a better bet as a batsman.

KENNETH HERVEY MacLEAY Born Bradford-on-Avon, Wiltshire, 2.4.59. RHB, RM. 16 LOI for Australia 1983-87. SFC: 27 matches; 844 runs @ 27.23; HS 74 v Warwickshire, Taunton, 1992; HT 427 in 1992; 34 wickets @ 34.79; BB 3-40 v Derbyshire, Derby, 1991; HT 25 in 1991. NWT: 4 matches; 33 runs @ 33.00; 4 wickets @ 36.50. BHC: 6 matches; 112 runs @ 18.67; 0 wickets. SL: 25 matches; 222 runs @ 17.08; 32 wickets @ 20.72. Western Australia 1981-90.

JOHN MARTIN
1964 - 1965

He had the fast bowler's build and picked up plenty of wickets to complement his three blues at Oxford. The good-natured story that persists is of the Minor Counties' match when the Somerset seamers were hammered mercilessly before lunch. Bill Andrews, in charge, had gone to the nearby Ring of Bells for a refresher and when he returned to the ground he said over lunch to the surprised undergraduate: "Let's admit it, John — you were bowling some rubbish out there." The reply was: "But I haven't bowled yet." To which Bill, never lost for words, came back: "Don't argue with me!"

JOHN DONALD MARTIN Born Oxford, 23.12.41. RHB, RFM. SFC: 2 matches; 0 runs; 3 wickets @ 43.00; BB 3-59 v Hampshire, Taunton, 1964. Oxford 1962-65.

John McMahon

JOHN McMAHON 1954 - 1957

Once he took eight wickets in an innings for Surrey; then he did the same for Somerset. This colourful, enigmatic Australian was a thoroughly capable left-arm slow bowler, who would cannily amend his style to suit the occasion. By 1956 he was taking 100 wickets for the county and the complaints that Hazell had been fired prematurely were allowed to die. His departure from Somerset, not apparently based on his deeds with the spinning ball, was an abrupt, unforgiving matter. Team-mates, who valued his uncomplicated, reliable slow bowling, fought in vain for a reversal of the decision.

JOHN WILLIAM JOSEPH McMAHON Born Balaclava, Australia, 28.12.17. RHB, SLA. Cap 1954. SFC: 115 matches; 645 runs @ 6.14; HS 24 v Sussex, Frome, 1955; HT 262 in 1955; 349 wickets @ 26.12; BB 8-46 v Kent, Yeovil, 1955; 100 wickets once; HT 103 in 1956. Surrey 1947-53.

NEIL MALLENDER 1987 -

Test recognition, when it came in 1992, was hardly expected. Twice he had been put on alert while on his customary playing-coaching stint in New Zealand. But it must have appeared increasingly as if his chance at the highest level would never arrive. When it did, he bowled as well as any of the more established England players — though he was forgotten again for the approaching winter tour. 'Ghost' (it's that pale complexion and fair hair) is highly regarded on the domestic circuit; in the clichés of the trade, he's the definitive honest workhorse. He bowls straight, he hits the seam. Yorkshire, his native county, let him slip away. He was ready to leave Northants. And Brian Rose, then manager and needing urgently to recruit additional bowlers, flew out to New Zealand to persuade Mallender to come back West (he'd once attended Yeovil Grammar School for a time, excelling at rugby and cricket). There aren't many better golfers who play cricket for a living. The benefit, awarded for 1994, was well earned. *Photo opposite.*

NEIL ALAN MALLENDER Born Kirk Sandall, Yorkshire, 13.8.61. RHB, RFM. Cap 1987. 2 Tests 1992. SFC: 110 matches; 1191 runs @ 16.54; HS 87* v Sussex, Hove, 1990; HT 250 in 1993; 313 wickets @ 25.18; BB 7-61 v Derbyshire, Taunton, 1987; HT 51 in 1990. NWT: 12 matches; 25 runs @12.50; 16 wickets @ 21.31. BHC: 29 matches; 68 runs @ 6.80; 37 wickets @ 29.95. SL: 83 matches; 363 runs @ 19.11; 78 wickets @ 30.09. Northamptonshire 1980-86. Otago, New Zealand, 1983-.

COLIN MITCHELL 1952 - 1954

This amiable amateur, who also captained the 2nd XI, once took six wickets in an innings at Frome. He was fast by club standards but he had work to think of, apart from cricket, back in Bristol. An outstanding local footballer, a left winger with a prolific scoring record, he played for Gloucestershire AFC over a number of years.

COLIN GERALD MITCHELL Born Brislington, Bristol, 27.1.29. RHB, RFM. Cap 1953. SFC: 30 matches; 186 runs @ 7.44; HS 26* v Worcestershire, Frome, 1953; 53 wickets @ 38.40; BB 6-62 same match; HT 47 in 1953.

Colin Mitchell

If anyone ever ran a popularity poll of all post-war players around the counties, this farmer's son would demand a lofty place. It wasn't simply that he walked away from petty or lacerating arguments, that he always chose to put the team before the individual, or that he retained a whimsical manner and schoolboyish giggle even in taut times. His generously endowed all-rounder's talents, which brought him six Tests and 34 one-day internationals, were contained in the most equable and self-effacing of personae (spelt in deference to Marks, the classical scholar).

He was part of Somerset's most successful and volatile team, probably the quietest. As an off-spinner, he tweaked those Chinnock fingers teasingly. When he was punished, the shoulders hunched and the consoling ciggies helped him through the lunch or tea interval. Soon he was smiling again, if privately wishing that the Taunton boundary fence had been less embracing to insensitive batsmen. He never much compromised his style in the one-day game and, significantly, could often be a match-winner. When it was his turn to bat, we knew he was worthy of more hundreds. He improvised when he had to, most effectively, an ungainly runner between the wickets.

Vic earned four blues at Oxford; now the deserved accolades come from his journalism. Captaincy came to him late, when Roebuck decided abruptly that he'd had enough. He wasn't in charge sufficiently long really for us to measure his worth in that onerous role. Man-management was no problem. He could shuffle his cards to meet a tactical challenge and was patently unselfish. But the ugly cold-steel blade of battle was not for him. Vic helped to bring his university friend Chris Tavare and manager Jack Birkenshaw to Somerset; he was also an influence on the arrival of Jimmy Cook. *Photo opposite.*

Norman Mitchell-Innes

VICTOR JAMES MARKS Born Middle Chinnock, Somerset, 25.6.55. RHB, OB. Cap 1979. Captain 1988-89. 6 Tests 1982-84. 34 LOI 1980-88. SFC: 275 matches; 9742 runs @ 30.54; 4 centuries; HS 134 v Worcestershire, Weston-super-Mare, 1984; 1000 runs twice; HT 1262 in 1984; 738 wickets @ 32.89; BB 8-17 v Lancashire, Bath, 1985; HT 86 in 1984. GC/NWT: 30 matches; 527 runs @ 31.00; 25 wickets @ 30.44; MoM 2. BHC: 49 matches; 790 runs @ 28.21; 46 wickets @ 31.91; GA 4. SL: 170 matches; 2299 runs @ 21.89; 154 wickets @ 26.01. Oxford 1975-78; Western Australia 1986-87.

NORMAN MITCHELL-INNES
1931 - 1949

Lucky he may have been to be chosen, when still an undergraduate, to play for England — and unlucky to be discarded soon after. He got his chance because Plum Warner vividly remembered 'Mandy's' jaunty 168 for Oxford against the South Africans in the May. In the Trent Bridge Test he flopped but was retained for Lord's. He had to withdraw because of chronic hay fever and was never asked again. Ironically, coinciding with the Lord's match, he suppressed his sneezes, batted down the order and scored a fine hundred again for Oxford. His duties in the Sudan Political Service restricted his cricket for Somerset, though he was one of the (many) captains in 1948. He was a mature, stylish batsman who, if he had been able to stay in this country, might have been quite an influence on county cricket. Apart from his cricket, he was a gifted golfer.

NORMAN STEWART MITCHELL-INNES Born Calcutta, India, 7.9.14. RHB, RFM. Cap pre-war. Joint Captain 1948. 1 Test 1935. SFC: 127 matches; 2835 runs @ 24.23; 3 centuries; HS 182 v Worcestershire, Kidderminster, 1936; HT 499 in 1936; 31 wickets @ 35.68; BB 4-65 v Sussex, Eastbourne, 1934. Oxford 1934-37.

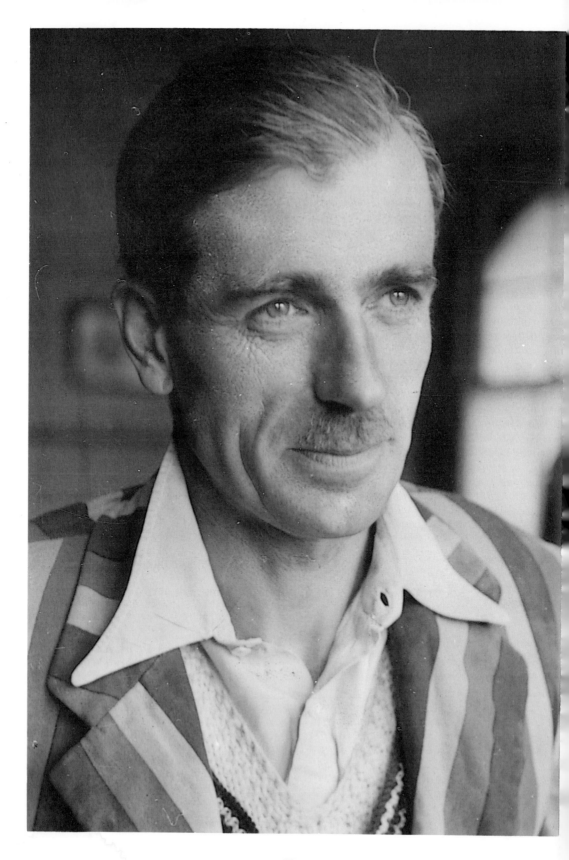

JACK MEYER
1936 - 1949

Innovative, experimental, eccentric: those three adjectives will do to begin with, in conveying the flavour of this tall, lean man who founded Millfield School. As an educationalist, he was an unorthodox visionary. He often operated on a 'Robin Hood' principle, stinging wealthy parents and enabling promising young sportsmen from humbler homes to have a comparatively inexpensive schooling. As a result, a formidable list of boys made it from the Millfield 1st XI to Somerset. Meyer's own appearances for the county were necessarily limited; by the time he was captaining them, for a summer in 1947, he was bent double by lumbago. Inevitably he led the team of slightly cynical pros with an endearing quirkiness that, in matters of field-placing for instance, could be quite bewildering. He was nonetheless a fine cricketer. His batting brought him one double-century, clinched allegedly by an offer of a donation to the opposing beneficiary's fund. His bowling could be a nightmare to any wicketkeeper; he spun the ball at brisk medium-pace, was proud of his late swing and liked to trifle with half a dozen variations in an over. He seldom went to bed, sleeping for a few hours instead in the headmaster's study. He liked placing a bet and kept a racing form-book with his academic tomes. In London he was known to spend all night at the gaming tables, alas at times with disastrous results. *Photo opposite.*

ROLLO JOHN OLIVER MEYER Born Ampthill, Bedfordshire, 15.3.05. RHB, RM. Cap pre-war. Captain 1947. SFC: 65 matches; 2929 runs @ 28.16; 2 centuries; HS 202* v Lancashire, Taunton, 1936; HT 853 in 1947; 158 wickets @ 28.32; BB 7-74 v Northamptonshire, Weston-super-Mare, 1947; HT 43 in 1947. Cambridge 1924-26; Bombay, Western India and Europeans, all in India, 1926-35. Died 9.3.91.

HALLAM MOSELEY
1971 - 1982

Around the Somerset grounds, he had a cult following — especially among the mums and the schoolchildren. For years his gentle affability was a golden plus in public relations. He had been recommended to the county by Sir Gary Sobers and, in a different decade, might have squeezed into the West Indian pace attack. The bowling action was one to be admired: he came in, spring-heeled and arm high, and the ball veered away towards the slips. Latterly the movement was

Hallam Moseley

less marked but the enthusiasm, as demonstrated in the sweet co-ordination of his fielding, never lessened. A sorry misunderstanding meant that he left in the end a season before he need have. He cherished an ambition to become a butcher but in later years he was to be seen as a peak-capped security officer in the London area.

HALLAM REYNOLD MOSELEY Born Christchurch, Barbados, 28.5.48. RHB, RFM. Cap 1972. SFC: 205 matches; 1502 runs @ 12.41; HS 67 v Leicestershire, Taunton, 1972; HT 234 in 1972; 547 wickets @ 24.10; BB 6-34 v Derbyshire, Bath, 1975; HT 81 in 1974. GC/NWT: 12 matches; 27 runs @ 4.50; 21 wickets @ 19.38. BHC: 47 matches; 128 runs @ 8.53; 66 wickets @ 19.58; SL: 151 matches; 364 runs @ 8.66; 222 wickets @ 20.23. Barbados, West Indies, 1969-72.

MUSHTAQ AHMED 1993 -

Here we had Merlin the Magician. Every delivery was a new trick, part of a sleight-of-hand miscellany to delight audiences round the country, many of them prepared to subjugate their partisanship and applaud his bewildering performances instead. With foresight and resourcefulness, Somerset announced him as their overseas signing for 1993. Soon, all were agreeing that there wasn't a better or more enthralling one to be found in the land.

He has brought a new dimension of pleasurable artifice to the domestic cricket scene. As the flaxen-haired Aussie, Shane Warne, confirmed, our first-class game has been denuded of wristy leg-tweakers for too long. Suddenly schoolboys are being encouraged to bowl them. Players like Mushtaq are their role-models.

His first season with Somerset was an unmitigated success. A few pitches were decidedly unfavourable to him, but he made the most of them and ended the summer not so far short of 100 first-class wickets. His top-spinners and flippers are an intriguing joy. The sheer variety of his output can be as demanding for wicketkeepers as batsmen. He enriched the championship with his presence. His cap, the only one awarded in 1993, was a formality. He won several matches virtually on his own. His demeanour revealed that he was always enjoying himself. At times he was the most perky of batsmen, mocking his small stature with effortless sixes out of the Taunton ground. From the days of Braund, through to schoolboy Cameron and little Lawrence, they have always appreciated cheeky leg-spinners down in the West Country. *Photo opposite.*

MUSHTAQ AHMED Born Sahiwal, Pakistan, 28.6.70. RHB, LBG. Cap 1993. 10 Tests 1990-. 70 LOI 1990-. SFC: 16 matches; 498 runs @ 19.92; HS 90 v Sussex, Taunton, 1993; 85 wickets @ 20.74; BB 7-91 v Sussex, Taunton, 1993. NWT: 4 matches; 54 runs @ 27.00; 5 wickets @ 27.20; MoM 1. BHC: 2 matches; 7 runs @ 7.00; 0 wickets. SL: 13 matches; 89 runs @ 8.09; 17 wickets @ 21.35. Multan United Bank, Pakistan, 1986-.

KERRY O'KEEFFE 1971 - 1972

One of those overseas players, barely known when he arrived, who went on to become a Test man. He played 24 times for Australia in the 1960s. He was a quickish leg-spinner, not easy to keep to (although Derek Taylor managed it well). There

Kerry O'Keeffe

was a high action and a useful top-spinner thrown in. But there was inconsistency, too, and he decided not to come back in 1973.

KERRY JAMES O'KEEFFE Born Sydney, Australia, 25.11.49. RHB, LBG. Cap 1971. 24 Tests 1971-77. 2 LOI 1977. SFC: 46 matches; 830 runs @ 20.75; HS 58 v Warwickshire, Glastonbury, 1971; HT 419 in 1972; 93 wickets @ 30.83; BB 7-38 v Sussex, Taunton, 1971; HT 74 in 1971. GC: 2 matches; 3 runs @ 1.50; 1 wicket @ 68.00. BHC: 3 matches; 17 runs @ 8.50; 3 wickets @ 41.33. SL: 15 matches; 131 runs @ 32.75; 4 wickets @ 25.25. New South Wales, Australia, 1968-80.

MARTIN OLIVE 1977 - 1981

Everyone liked the look of his batting at Millfield. He made his county debut as a teenager — a stylish, promising presence at the wicket, a pleasant personality  away from it. It was difficult, though, for a newcomer to break in and establish himself at that particular time. Moved to Devon to work for a building society, eventfully. The premises were held up on his first day there.

MARTIN OLIVE Born Watford, Hertfordshire, 18.4.58. RHB. SFC: 17 matches; 467 runs @ 15.57; HS 50 v Yorkshire, Weston-super-Mare, 1980; HT 290 in 1980. SL: 1 match; 2 runs (no average).

Richard Ollis

RICHARD OLLIS   1981 - 1985

This upright left-hander was once stranded on 99 against Gloucestershire at Bristol. Home skipper David Graveney did his best, successfully, to fiddle an extra over for the batsman, but the necessary single still eluded him. Maybe he didn't realise what was happening.

RICHARD LESLIE OLLIS Born Clifton, Bristol, 14.1.61. LHB, RM. SFC: 37 matches; 1016 runs @ 18.14; HS 99* v Gloucestershire, Bristol, 1983; HT 517 in 1983; 0 wickets. BHC: 4 matches; 39 runs @ 13.00. SL: 11 matches; 75 runs @ 12.50.

Gary Palmer

GARY PALMER   1982 - 1989

Did the fact that he was Ken's son work against him? It's impossible to tell. Somerset had enthusiastically monitored his progress from school to 2nd XI level. With fatuously premature judgment, some pundits viewed the 16-year-old and argued that here might be the next Botham. He was a great trier, a lively bowler with an odd action, and not a bad batsman. But perhaps too much was expected of him. He was squeezed out by other young bowlers like Davis and his progress sadly tailed away.

GARY VINCENT PALMER Born Taunton, 1.11.65. RHB, RMF. SFC: 54 matches; 903 runs @ 15.31; HS 78 v Gloucestershire, Bristol, 1983; HT 299 in 1984; 92 wickets @ 44.64; BB 5-38 v Warwickshire, Taunton, 1983; HT 30 in 1984. NWT: 4 matches; 27 runs @ 27.00; 4 wickets @ 33.50. BHC: 10 matches; 81 runs @ 16.20; 8 wickets @ 39.75. SL: 63 matches; 294 runs @ 16.33; 60 wickets @ 28.30.

KEN PALMER   1955 - 1969

There were times that he gave the impression that he was carrying the cares of the world on his shoulders. In fact, on occasions he did carry the Somerset attack. His record for the county is not to be under-valued. He was after all the first member of the West Country club since the war to complete the double, in 1961. By consistently hitting the seam and obtaining some swing away from the bat, he took 100 wickets four times. When the strip was greenish he pounded away like a pugnacious terrier. That was when one could detect the challenge in his eye.

Yet he was given his first contract, as a teenager for Somerset, on the strength of his batting. He liked to open the innings then. Successive coaches Harry Parks and Horace Hazell had seen enough to recommend him. He was a ready listener, though much of the early tuition and encouragement had come from his father, who worked as a groundsman at Roundway Hospital, Devizes. Young Kenny had actually been born in Hampshire and had gone to Southampton for a trial. His mind was set on county cricket. Even as a lad his attitude was doggedly determined. He hated giving his wicket away; he cast a scathing glance down 22 yards when a batsman hit him for four.

His scintillating all-round form of 1961 was never quite repeated. But an unlikely Test

Photo opposit

opportunity did come, four years later. He was doing some coaching in Johannesburg at the time — and the England bowlers out in South Africa were running into all kinds of injury scares. The call went out and Palmer was rushed to Port Elizabeth for the fifth Test. There was no romantically successful sequel, even if he was handed the new ball. His one wicket from the two innings was earned at considerable expense — and then they put him to bat at No. 11. Hadn't they heard of his Devizes prowess at the top of the order? His best innings was at Northampton; he once nearly ran through the whole of the Notts side at Trent Bridge. After his playing career came the umpiring and Test status.

KENNETH ERNEST PALMER Born Winchester, Hampshire, 22.4.37. RHB, RFM. Cap 1958. 1 Test 1965. SFC: 302 matches; 7567 runs @ 20.73; 2 centuries; HS 125* v Northamptonshire, Northampton, 1961; 1000 runs once; HT 1036 in 1961; Double once in 1961; 837 wickets @ 21.11; BB 9-57 v Nottinghamshire, Trent Bridge, 1963; 100 wickets 4 times; HT 126 in 1963. GC: 14 matches; 109 runs @ 12.11; 23 wickets @ 19.60; MoM 1. SL: 10 matches; 28 runs @ 5.60; 11 wickets @ 25.64. Fc umpire 1972-.

ROY PALMER   1965 - 1970

The taller brother of Ken was a useful man to have around in the one-day game, as he demonstrated with a Sunday hat-trick, the final three deliveries, against Gloucestershire at Bristol. He saved his best championship cricket for Lord's. Once at Bath he ran into trouble for seam-picking. "He wasn't in the same class as Ken," joked a contemporary mischievously. Roy is also a successful umpire now. What was that expression about poachers and gamekeepers?

ROY PALMER Born Devizes, Wiltshire, 12.7.42. RHB, RFM. Cap 1969. SFC: 74 matches; 1037 runs @ 13.29; HS 84 v Leicestershire, Taunton, 1967; HT 275 in 1968; 172 wickets @ 31.62; BB 6-45 v Middlesex, Lord's, 1967; HT 60 in 1969. GC: 14 matches; 30 runs @ 2.73; 30 wickets @ 17.73; MoM 2. SL: 29 matches; 168 runs @ 9.88; 37 wickets @ 26.03. Fc umpire 1980-.

JIM PARKS   1973 - 1976

His highest score, a double-century, was for Sussex against Somerset. And when he said a somewhat unloving farewell to Hove, it was to Taunton he headed, persuaded by Brian Close. They needed him for some extra experience and to prop the higher order. He obliged with 1,000 runs in his first season with Somerset. His continuing role as wicketkeeper was a bone of

Roy Palmer

contention at Sussex. Ironically, Somerset already had Derek Taylor and Jim accepted that he was going to be needed as a stumper primarily for one-day matches. He had met Brian Close on tour in Rhodesia and been persuaded not to give up county cricket, as seemed likely, for a year or two. His valedictory summers with Somerset were relaxed and enjoyable.

JAMES MICHAEL PARKS Born Haywards Heath, Sussex, 21.10.31. RHB, LB, WK. Cap 1973. 46 Tests 1954-68. SFC: 47 matches; 1940 runs @ 30.31; 1 century; HS 155 v Kent, Maidstone, 1973; 1000 runs once; HT 1033 in 1973; 0 wickets; 2 dismissals (2 ct). GC: 3 matches; 69 runs @ 69.00. BHC: 10 matches; 214 runs @ 26.75; GA 1. SL: 27 matches; 444 runs @ 22.20.

Jim Parks

DEFINITELY A DRY BLACKTHORN DAY

How's that?

SOUTH WEST WATER

Peninsula House, Rydon Lane, Exeter EX2 7HR. Tel. (0392) 446688

Kevin (left) and Keith Parsons

KEVIN PARSONS · 1992 -

Worked in the county office during the winter of 1992-93 while his twin, Keith, went to New Zealand. It was a rare separation for two dedicated young players, able to show their skills and enthusiasm at the early, progressive levels.

KEVIN JOHN PARSONS Born Taunton, 2.5.73. RHB. OB. SL: 2 matches; 22 runs @ 22.00.

KEITH PARSONS · 1992 -

His cricket career had run identically with twin Kevin's. But Keith's chance came first, a fairly anonymous appearance against the Pakistan tourists in 1992. There followed his championship debut in 1993 and a handful of matches when he was given a chance in the middle-order. Like so many, Keith, a tidy bat and medium-paced seamer, discovered the gulf between the 2nd XI, where in his case the runs came productively, and first-class cricket. There were still encouraging aspects of his play, like the mature way he killed Ian Salisbury's leg-spin, to win approval from Bob Cottam. Whether at Taunton Deane or the County Ground, he has been, like Kevin, an eager learner.

KEITH ALAN PARSONS Born Taunton, 2.5.73. RHB. RM. SFC: 6 matches; 135 runs @ 13.50; HS 63 v Sussex, Taunton, 1993. 134 in 1993. 0 wickets. NWT: 2 matches; 33 runs @ 33.00; 2 wickets @ 23.50. SL: 7 matches; 83 runs @ 11.86; 1 wicket @ 49.00.

RICHARD PAULL · 1963 - 1964

He was a neat stroke-maker and a prospect. He shaped well in 2nd XI matches for Somerset. At Millfield the runs came attractively. But there were to be just six first-class matches for Somerset before he went off and got a blue at Cambridge.

RICHARD KENYON PAULL Born Bridgwater, 20.2.44. RHB. SFC: 6 matches; 104 runs @ 13.00; HS 21* v Sussex, Glastonbury, 1964. Cambridge 1967.

Richard Paull

Andrew Payne

Tony Pearson

ANDREW PAYNE 1992 -

This young Lancashire all-rounder, already eyed by one or two other counties, was signed by Bob Cottam. His form on Under-19 tours was encouraging. And, although he found championship selection elusive in 1992, he did compile a half-century on his debut. Progress over the following summer was quietly discernible and he gave the impression that he was part of Somerset's future. His own confidence must surely have been boosted when he caused a stir by dismissing Graham Gooch twice during a 2nd XI fixture.

ANDREW PAYNE Born Rossendale, Lancashire, 20.10.73. RHB, RM. SFC: 3 matches; 90 runs @ 90.00; HS 51* v Gloucestershire, Taunton, 1992 (debut); 4 wickets @ 15.50; BB 2-15 v Worcestershire, Worcester, 1993. SL: 12 matches; 116 runs @ 14.50; 6 wickets @ 59.00.

TONY PEARSON 1961 - 1963

We go to his Cambridge days (three blues) for his most memorable performance. At Loughborough in 1961, against Leicestershire, he took all ten for 78 runs. His obvious link with Somerset can be attributed to his schooling — and cricketing successes — at Downside. He bowled well above medium, possessing some natural swing. After half a dozen spaced appearances, and one fine stint against Worcestershire, he got on with a medical career.

ANTHONY JOHN GRAYHURST PEARSON Born Harrow, Middlesex, 30.12.41. RHB, RFM. SFC: 6 matches; 17 runs (no average); HS 15* v Kent, Gillingham, 1963; 26 wickets @ 19.50; BB 7-63 v Worcestershire, Bristol Imperial, 1961. Cambridge 1961-63.

RICHARD PETERS 1946

Just one match, after being well recommended at a time of selection uncertainties in the first season after the war, but the call was not apparently repeated.

RICHARD CHARLES PETERS Born Chew Magna, Somerset, 12.9.11. RHB, RF. SFC: 1 match; 5 runs @ 5.00; HS 3 v Leicestershire, Melton Mowbray, 1946; 0 wickets.

LEWIS PICKLES

One of the quite formidable contingent that came down from Yorkshire in that tentative post-war period. He shaped like a capable lad from those northern parts — and scored 1,000 runs in his first summer with Somerset. That kind of progress wasn't sustained, though in the second season he seemed worth the maiden hundred he desperately wanted, but didn't get, against Lancashire at Old Trafford.

LEWIS PICKLES Born Wakefield, Yorkshire, 17.9.32. RHB, OB. Cap 1956. SFC: 47 matches; 1702 runs @ 20.51; HS 87 v Lancashire, Old Trafford, 1956; 1000 runs once; HT 1137 in 1956; 1 wicket @ 65.00; BB 1-22 v Kent, Bath, 1956.

NIGEL POPPLEWELL   1979 - 1985

His Somerset contract followed a lively, fighting innings for Cambridge when they were bowled out for fewer than 100 at Bath. For the county he was apt to be jokey, self-deprecating and under-dressed (though the appearance noticeably smartened when he was embraced by the legal profession). His cricket, early on, was inclined to be a trifle cavalier. But the wholeheartedness was always there. He was maybe no more than a modest bowler; his fielding could be brilliant, and his batting pleasantly adaptable. He would open the innings, by then tighter in technique, and enjoyed the role even more when he was on his toes to execute the square-cut which proved most profitable to him. Those who saw his 172 at Southend described it as exquisite. Those who saw his hundred in 41 minutes at Bath recalled his jocular behaviour the previous night on a narrow boat when he was playfully pushed into the Avon by Ian Botham. The trend of the game ("it had become less gentle and joyful") brought signs of disenchantment. It was time to put on a suit and follow in his illustrious father's footsteps.

NIGEL FRANCIS MARK POPPLEWELL Born Chislehurst, Kent, 8.8.57. RHB, RM. Cap 1983. SFC: 118 matches; 4594 runs @ 28.18; 4 centuries; HS 172 v Essex, Southend, 1985; 1000 runs twice; HT 1116 in 1984; 78 wickets @ 39.60; BB 5-33 v Northamptonshire, Weston-super-Mare, 1981; HT 23 in 1983. NWT: 14 matches; 297 runs @ 27.00; 4 wickets @ 31.75; MoM 1. BHC: 22 matches; 365 runs @ 22.81; 4 wickets @ 46.00; GA 2. SL: 79 matches; 1360 runs @ 24.72; 34 wickets @ 28.97. Cambridge 1977-79.

Lewis Pickles

Nigel Popplewell

VIV RICHARDS
1974 - 1986

How do we measure genius? Does it have to be so soullessly perfect that it doesn't allow fallibility? Surely not. Richards made mistakes at the wicket; he would flash that Jumbo too early, as if still back at the grammar school in St John's, and give the bowler a chance. He would appear to rewrite the manuals by clipping the ball just outside off stump through mid-wicket. He'd lapse in concentration and the thrilling instincts of the automatic pilot would let him down. But for much of the time he ruled supreme. At Taunton, where he had arrived from his Lansdown qualification, wide-eyed and shyly charming, he regularly put the ball over the old pavilion roof as if he were merely golf-chipping. The wondrous eyesight in those days enabled him to pick up the flight of the ball quicker than anyone else in the game. His feet and his timing mocked any murmur of criticism at his tendency to veer from the purest orthodoxy. The rate of his scoring, never bolstered by an ugly slog, made him quickly a Somerset idol; even the forward defensive seemed to go for four.

Was it too good to last? Some misinterpreted the natural swagger in the walk. The eyes gradually became more wary, the persona seemingly more cynical. He had become a great global cricketer. But captaincy of his own country was delayed and he appeared at times to be victim of inter-island differences. The fuse had always been short — hadn't he once smashed his bat into a thousand pieces in self-rebuke and frustration on the stone floor of the dressing room? Hadn't he once jumped the boundary fence to confront a bigot? Racial pride was his driving force. At times there were too many words in his ear, too many prejudices being awakened, too much advice being offered. Rejection by Somerset, as he saw it, was the final and cruellest ignominy. He would never forgive. We should shut out, in our memories, his bitterness and the wrath in his voice. Remember the acclaim he brought modest Antigua; the effortless ferocity of his hitting; the brutally brilliant triple-hundred which caused disbelieving Warwickshire players to say, in admiration and despair, that they might as well give up the game for good; the awesome fielding; the quiet conviviality of his happier days. After leaving Somerset, he had a season with Rishton in the league and then enjoyable years with Glamorgan. *Photo opposite.*

ISAAC VIVIAN ALEXANDER RICHARDS Born St John's, Antigua, 7.3.52. RHB, OB. Cap 1974. 121 Tests 1974 - 1991. 187 LOI 1975-91. SFC: 191 matches; 14698 runs @ 49.82; 47 centuries; HS 322 v Warwickshire, Taunton, 1985; 1000 runs 10 times; HT 2161 in 1977; 96 wickets @ 44.16; BB 4-36 v Derbyshire, Chesterfield, 1986; HT 16 in 1982. GC/NWT: 31 matches; 1209 runs @ 43.17; 16 wickets @ 29.88; MoM 4. BHC: 43 matches; 1395 runs @ 42.27; 7 wickets @ 32.14; GA 6. SL: 144 matches; 4745 runs @ 38.57; 70 wickets @ 25.11. Glamorgan 1990-93. Leeward and Combined Islands, West Indies, 1971-. Queensland, Australia, 1976-77.

Nick Pringle

NICK PRINGLE
1986 - 1991

Was it basically a lack of self-confidence? Or even a lack of opportunities? The promise, going back to Taunton School days, had been evident enough. He had a neat technique and was a nimble fielder. When he left Somerset, the understandable hope was that he might find another county.

NICHOLAS JOHN PRINGLE Born Weymouth, Dorset, 20.9.66. RHB, RMF. SFC: 27 matches; 707 runs @ 16.83; HS 79 v Warwickshire, Edgbaston, 1987; HT 347 in 1987; 5 wickets @ 110.20; BB 2-35 v Glamorgan, Weston-super-Mare, 1987. NWT: 1 match; 17 runs @ 17.00. SL: 11 matches; 80 runs @ 10.00; 0 wickets.

JOHN ROBERTS
1969 - 1970

In he came, thick-set and determined, at left-arm medium over the wicket. He had come down from the North with a nice Scouse sense of humour. After two years it was mutually decided that he was not going to be the answer and he changed direction to patrol the beat for the police instead.

JOHN KELVIN ROBERTS Born Liverpool, 9.10.49. RHB, LM. SFC: 8 matches; 3 runs @ 1.00; HS 2* v Yorkshire, Headingley, 1969; 15 wickets @ 32.33; BB 4-38 same match; HT 14 in 1969. SL: 11 matches; 13 runs @ 13.00; 13 wickets @ 22.85.

Jim Redman

for Worcester City and later Taunton Town. And although by then well into his twenties, Bristol City once showed distinct interest. He went on to guide and encourage many 2nd XI players and become the most conscientious of coaches for Somerset. *Photo opposite.*

PETER JAMES ROBINSON Born Worcester, 9.2.43. LHB, SLA. Cap 1966. SFC: 180 matches; 4887 runs @ 21.53; 3 centuries; HS 140 v Northamptonshire, Northampton, 1970; 1000 runs once; HT 1158 in 1970; 291 wickets @ 27.38; BB 7-10 v Nottinghamshire, Trent Bridge, 1966; HT 70 in 1966. GC: 12 matches; 286 runs @ 28.60; 2 wickets @ 1.00. SL: 47 matches; 654 runs @ 22.55; 3 wickets @ 21.66. Worcestershire 1963-64.

JIM REDMAN   1948 - 1953

Frome produced its moments of personal glory, as the county's record books reveal. Jim's came here, against Derbyshire. He'd never produced so much movement and was at times almost unplayable as he took his seven cheap wickets. For the most part, he was an artisan seamer — persevering but unmemorable. There were also some useful bowling stints for Wiltshire.

JAMES REDMAN Born Bath, 1.3.26. RHB, RMF. Cap 1951. SFC: 65 matches; 1012 runs @ 12.34; HS 45 v Essex, Brentwood, 1951; HT 472 in 1951; 117 wickets @ 35.63; BB 7-23 v Derbyshire, Frome, 1951; HT 50 in 1951. Died 24.9.81.

PETER ROBINSON   1965 - 1977

There were too many similar bowlers at Worcestershire so he decided it made sense in moving to Somerset, for whom he took nearly 300 wickets and, with an efficient if restricted repertoire, scored three hundreds. He's the nephew of Roly Jenkins, who passed on humour, wisdom and the craftsmanship of the slow bowler's trade. Peter could be relied on to pitch the ball with precision, a nagger that batsmen forced with difficulty. With the bat, he would open the innings if necessary with doughty resolve — as he did in the 1967 Gillette final against Kent. He was not far short of becoming a professional footballer; he played outstandingly

ELLIS ROBINSON   1950 - 1952

It was perhaps too much to expect his spinning fingers to contain the same wizardry for Somerset as they did for Yorkshire before and after the war. Yet his consistent off-breaks could still bring him 100 wickets in a season after coming West and, once at Weston, he returned match figures of 15-78. He remained a North Countryman by nature, not wholly approving of differing attitudes in Somerset. He went on tour to Jamaica with Yorkshire in the mid-1930s; some felt he deserved greater recognition in the years that followed.

ELLIS PEMBROKE ROBINSON Born Denaby Main, Yorkshire, 10.8.11. LHB, ROB. Cap 1950. SFC: 89 matches; 867 runs @ 8.18; HS 40 v Lancashire, Bath, 1950; HT 369 in 1950; 256 wickets @ 28.55; BB 8-47 v Sussex, Weston-super-Mare, 1951; 100 wickets once; HT 107 in 1951. Yorkshire 1934-49.

Ellis Robinson

RAY ROBINSON
1964

One match — and not a run to show for it. Better known as the Taunton and Somerset rugby player and father of Bath's international, Andy.

RAYMOND THOMAS ROBINSON Born Charmouth, Dorset, 15.9.40. RHB. SFC: 1 match; 0 runs.

Brian Roe

BRIAN ROE
1957 - 1966

The defence was dogged, the personality amiable. 'Chico' was one of the smallest players on the circuit, causing older ladies on the West Country boundaries to feel they wanted to mother him. In fact, he could always look after himself pretty well, especially against the fast bowlers. He relished opening the innings and worked hard for his four centuries. In the end there was rather too much competition for places. So he opened for Devon instead.

BRIAN ROE Born Cleethorpes, Lincolnshire, 27.1.39. RHB. Cap 1962. SFC: 131 matches; 4859 runs @ 22.39; 4 centuries; HS 128 v Essex, Brentwood, 1962; 1000 runs 3 times; HT 1552 in 1962; 2 wickets @ 52,00; BB 1-43 v Yorkshire, Taunton, 1961. GC: 5 matches; 55 runs @ 11.00.

PETER ROEBUCK
1974 - 1991

The history of the game of cricket is littered with the names of those who fell out of love with it. Many confined their feelings to confidants or only said so in retrospective contemplation. Roebuck went public. He got out at the age of 35, when there were plenty of runs left in him, because he argued that cricket had become too cynical and results were being manufactured. And yes, he admitted, he didn't much enjoy being a foot soldier after his days as a general. That was an honest observation on playing under Tavare, just an anonymous fielder and rarely consulted by the new captain. The relationship never smouldered with antipathy but it was sterile, mutually unproductive. 'Rupert' likened it perceptively to an arts-science divide (he was arts!).

He first played for Somerset 2nd XI at the age of 13. Only three batsmen made more first-class runs for the county, just two — Gimblett and Richards — scored more hundreds. Roebuck never had as many shots as they, admitting he could look boring because of it. In truth he worked hard to increase his range and was capable of emerging with the most pleasant of drives and cuts. His application made him invaluable in a crisis on difficult wickets. He had courage, physical as well as moral, as he took on the new ball. We shall never quite discover how he failed, when England were patently looking for a grafter, to make a Test appearance or two. He was also sized up as a possible captain. Was he too opinionated? Did he possess too many whims?

Introspective, cerebral, moody, self-contained: he was all these things. He was also a dependable cricketer and team man, an imaginative tactician and a captain who refused to dispense clichés. Because of the position he held and the views he intrepidly expressed, he took much of the flak, as a leading antagonist, when the decision was taken to fire Richards and Garner. He was physically threatened by one of the departing stars and called 'Judas' by another. But he stuck to his well-reasoned brief, as one would expect of someone with a First in Law at Cambridge. His literary skills had always been evident; now he turned full-time to journalism, while establishing himself as a successful author, with a most comprehensive and readable history of his county club among his growing number of books. There have also been hints that he could essay plays, just like a Somerset predecessor George Nichols, and even politics. *Photo opposite.*

PETER MICHAEL ROEBUCK Born Oxford, 6.3.56. RHB, LB. Cap 1978. Captain 1986-88. SFC: 306 matches; 16212 runs @ 38.33; 31 centuries; HS 221* v Nottinghamshire, Trent Bridge, 1986; 1000 runs 9 times; HT 1702 in 1984; 45 wickets @ 54.27; BB 3-10 v Leicestershire, Weston-super-Mare, 1991; HT 11 in 1989. GC/NWT: 38 matches; 1087 runs @ 31.06; 3 wickets @ 46.33; MoM 2. BHC: 57 matches; 1498 runs @ 31.88; 8 wickets @ 25.88; GA 2. SL: 180 matches; 4191 runs @ 29.31; 28 wickets @ 21.71. Cambridge 1975-77.

Stuart Rogers

STUART ROGERS 1948 - 1953

The question used to be: where do we find an old-style amateur, one with time on his hands and an affection for cricket? Rogers's appointment took most West Countrymen by surprise. They didn't necessarily disapprove of his loose, lively and technically naive batting, but they soon suspected that his tactical sense was suspect. He filled the captaincy gap for three years; in that time he scored three hundreds and leaned a bit on his senior pros like Horace Hazell, taken off in the skipper's flashy sports car occasionally for an evening meal and strong claret (until then an alien drink for the earthy spinner). Rogers's approach could be attractively cavalier but some of the younger professionals wished he'd got to know them better.

STUART SCOTT ROGERS Born Muswell Hill, London, 18.3.23. RHB. Cap 1949. Captain 1950-52. SFC: 118 matches; 3607 runs @ 19.08; 3 centuries; HS 107* v South Africans, Taunton, 1951; 1000 runs once; HT 1127 in 1950; 2 wickets @ 63.00; BB 2-13 v Nottinghamshire, Trent Bridge, 1950. Madras Europeans, India, 1946-47. Died 6.5.69.

BRIAN ROSE 1969 - 1987

Initially he wasn't everyone's idea of a long-term prospect, so he went off to qualify as a teacher instead. Later, his appointment as captain didn't find favour in all quarters. History showed him to be a sound skipper and the leader of the county in its most memorable summers when trophies at last came to Taunton. He was in charge of a team which included players of exceptional talent and high profile, a task which could be rewarding and on occasions unenviable. He was a private person and was apt to carry a preoccupied expression onto the field. Tongue-in-cheek team-mates suspected aloud that he was probably just as happy doing his beloved gardening.

His batting could be of high calibre. As a left-hander at the top of the order, his strokes were stylish and crisp. He belonged to Weston-super-Mare and it was appropriate that he should have hit a double-century there. When Alec Bedser once came west to take a detailed look at Botham, he returned home rhapsodising about Rose instead. There were nine Test appearances but also untimely injuries in his career. Mental pain, too, after that highly controversial Benson and Hedges match in 1979, when Somerset were dismissed from the competition for 'bending the rules'. A sensitive man, who continued to maintain that nothing illegal had been done, he was stunned by the weight of ire from the game's establishment.

Some believed that he could have proved himself a genuine all-rounder. At medium-pace, with some natural swing, he once took three wickets in four balls at headquarters. But he chose to stick to his batting. He was tactically sharp, as well as a reliable judge of talent. These qualities served him well as unofficial manager of the county club and as chairman of the cricket committee. *Photo opposite.*

BRIAN CHARLES ROSE Born Dartford, Kent, 4.6.50. LHB, LM. Cap 1975. Captain 1978-83. 9 Tests 1977-81. 2 LOI 1977. SFC: 251 matches; 12342 runs @ 33.27; 23 centuries; HS 205 v Northamptonshire, Weston-super-Mare, 1977; 1000 runs 8 times; HT 1624 in 1976; 8 wickets @ 36.13; BB 3-9 v Gloucestershire, Taunton, 1975. GC/NWT: 26 matches; 757 runs @ 37.85; MoM 2. BHC: 53 matches; 1342 runs @ 30.50; GA 2. SL: 172 matches; 3609 runs @ 25.77; 7 wickets @ 21.71.

GRAHAM ROSE   1987 -

He arrived in 1987 as Somerset recruited anxiously, attempting to fill the gaps left by the famous. The shoulders were broad, the stride was long, making him appear more Creech St Michael than Tottenham St Venables, his favoured native habitat. The unquestionable promise of the all-rounder has not yet quite been fulfilled. With that height and thrust, his bowling can carry deceptive pace and bounce on good days. But it is his batting that, with the right persuasion and in the right circumstances, can transform a match. He can drive hard, high and straight. The century off 36 balls at Torquay in the NatWest set a new record for the competition. Here is a Londoner capable of sustaining the ever-appreciated big-hitting Somerset tradition.

GRAHAM DAVID ROSE Born Tottenham, London, 12.4.64. RHB, RMF. Cap 1988. SFC: 132 matches; 4498 runs @ 31.45; 5 centuries; HS 138 v Sussex, Taunton, 1993; 1000 runs once; HT 1000 in 1990; 291 wickets @ 30.97; BB 6-47 v Warwickshire, Bath, 1988; HT 57 in 1988. NWT: 13 matches; 252 runs @ 22.91; 15 wickets @ 25.87. BHC: 33 matches; 530 runs @ 23.04; 42 wickets @ 28.36; GA 2. SL: 95 matches; 1946 runs @ 29.04; 103 wickets @ 24.89. Middlesex 1985-86.

Graham Rose

FRED RUMSEY   1963 - 1968

His value to the county, whatever the whims and extrovert flourish, is seen even better at this distance. At Worcestershire he had done little of note, squeezed out by the regular fast bowlers. So he came to Somerset, on special registration, and astonished most people — especially those from his former county — by taking 100 wickets. Before long he was making five Test appearances and arguably deserving more.

Here was a real fast bowler, left-arm at that, who could make some batsmen quake. He needed to be used in shortish bursts, to be handled intelligently on and off the field, to be appreciated for the vision he often imparted to the conversation. During his six years with Somerset the girth broadened and the arm got lower. The expanse of the heart seldom lessened. He and Palmer, in tandem with the new ball, gave the county hope. The ideas kept pace with the wicked deliveries. He spoke up for professional sportsmen and was the man behind the formation of the Cricketers' Association in 1967. For a short time he helped Somerset with their public relations, before extending the role with Derbyshire. Then followed a burgeoning career in travel and corporate hospitality. It should be added that Fred liked to dine well himself. *Photo opposite.*

FREDERICK EDWARD RUMSEY Born Stepney, London, 4.12.35. RHB, LF. Cap 1963. 5 Tests 1964-65. SFC: 153 matches; 766 runs @ 7.66; HS 45 v Sussex, Weston-super-Mare, 1967; HT 154 in 1963; 520 wickets @ 19.79; BB 8-26 v Hampshire, Bath, 1965; 100 wickets twice; HT 102 in 1963. GC: 15 matches; 9 runs @ 4.50; 30 wickets @ 11.37. Worcestershire 1960-62; Derbyshire 1970.

NEIL RUSSOM   1980 - 1983

There was some useful form at Cambridge and, one imagined, the possibility of a county career. The considered opinion at Taunton was that, although a good-looking bat and reasonable seamer, he was one of the many who over the years suffered from being around 'at the wrong time'.

NEIL RUSSOM Born Finchley, London, 3.12.58. RHB, RMF. SFC: 4 matches; 41 runs @ 13.67; HS 12 and 12* v Worcestershire, Weston-super-Mare, 1981; 5 wickets @ 33.00; BB 2-18 same match. SL: 1 match, did not bat or bowl. Cambridge 1979-81.

JOHN SAINSBURY — 1951

A county rugby player — but only two nominal appearances for his native Somerset at cricket. His best form was revealed for Clifton and club sides.

JOHN POPHAM SAINSBURY Born Axbridge, Somerset, 8.1.27. RHB, LM. SFC: 2 matches; 16 runs @ 4.00; HS 16 v Sussex, Weston-super-Mare, 1951.

TIM SCRIVEN — 1988 - 1989

Did well enough for Bucks against Somerset for the West Country club to show interest. Some wondered whether the county's search for a slow left-arm spinner had ended with this tall newcomer's arrival. Alas, three matches only.

TIMOTHY JOHN ADAM SCRIVEN Born High Wycombe, Buckinghamshire, 15.12.65. RHB, SLA. SFC: 3 matches; 11 runs @ 5.50; HS 7 v Derbyshire, Weston-super-Mare, 1988; 7 wickets @ 56.00; BB 2-67 v Lancashire, Taunton, 1989.

'ALAN' SHIRREFF — 1958

The ex-Squadron Leader had led RAF and Combined Services, and no doubt some saw him as ending up captain of Somerset. He arrived as assistant secretary, with some coaching responsibilities. It was never going to work. His face didn't fit in some quarters and there was an uneasy relationship between him and skipper Tremlett. He had come by way of Cambridge, Hampshire and Kent — but he had only two matches for Somerset, and didn't get a bowl.

ALEXANDER CAMPBELL SHIRREFF Born Ealing, London, 12.2.19. RHB. SFC: 2 matches; 47 runs @ 15.67; HS 24 v Essex, Taunton, 1958. Cambridge 1939; Hampshire 1946-47; Kent 1950-56.

JAKE SEAMER — 1932 - 1948

Son of a Somerset clergyman, Jake had a beaky ecclesiastical look himself. He was also a bit of a character, with a few surprises to enliven an away fixture. Appearances for the county were limited to leave periods from the Sudan Political Service. But he was one of the seemingly numerous Somerset skippers during 1948, when he endeared himself to most of the pros — for his persona rather than mere sporting ability. While at Oxford he once got spectacularly to nearly 200 against Minor Counties. He liked going for his shots, though in county cricket he always seemed to find himself as the willing and admiring foil to the muscular Wellard.

JOHN WEMYSS SEAMER Born Shapwick, Somerset, 23.6.13. RHB. Cap pre-war. Joint Captain 1948. SFC: 59 matches; 1405 runs @ 15.61; HS 70 v Derbyshire, Taunton, 1932; HT 291 in 1938; 0 wickets. Oxford 1933-36.

Jake Seamer

Dennis Silk

Phil Slocombe

DENNIS SILK   1956 - 1960

He was one of the country's top and most
respected headmasters — as Warden of Radley —
and after retiring to his beloved Somerset, he
became president of MCC. He's a man of gentle
voice, charm and authority: and if he hadn't put
education first, he'd have been unanimous choice
as captain of Somerset. The personality had the
right mix of leader and convivial companion, as
demonstrated on his various MCC tours, and for
two of which, to North America and New Zealand,
he was the skipper. His reliability as a batsman
and short-leg was evident from Cambridge days.
One only of his seven hundreds was for Somerset
but as a vacation player he was always worth his
place. So he was as a rugby man, at university,
Bath and county level.

DENNIS RAOUL WHITEHALL SILK Born Eureka, California,
8.10.31. RHB, LB. Cap 1957. SFC: 33 matches; 1543 runs @ 33.54;
1 century; HS 106* v Glamorgan, Cardiff, 1956; HT 525 in 1957; 0
wickets. Cambridge 1952-55.

PHIL SLOCOMBE   1975 - 1983

The promise was immense. A century came in his
third championship match and 1,000 runs in his
first season. The MCC selected him and his name
was firmly pencilled in for potential Test
inclusion before too long. Alas, fulfilment — and
latterly even selection — was elusive. Confidence
evaporated and, probably in desperation, he
became increasingly theoretical, opening his
stance and forsaking some of the neater, more
natural traits of the young Weston and Millfield
batsman. But he never lost his exquisite footwork
against the slow bowlers and could play spinners
like a dream. In the end, dejected by lessening
encouragement, he turned to antiques for a living.

PHILIP ANTHONY SLOCOMBE Born Weston-super-Mare, 6.9.54.
RHB, RM. Cap 1978. SFC: 135 matches; 5541 runs @ 27.84; 7
centuries; HS 132 v Nottinghamshire, Taunton, 1975; 1000 runs
twice; HT 1221 in 1978; 3 wickets @ 18.00; BB 1-2 v Gloucestershire,
Bristol, 1982. GC/NWT: 11 matches; 147 runs @ 18.38. BHC: 11
matches; 109 runs @ 10.90. SL: 56 matches; 573 runs @ 15.07.

ROY SMITH 1949 - 1955

Not enough happened in the painstaking, unspectacular career of local boy Smith, whose left-arm slows were accurate enough but didn't give experienced batsmen too much trouble. His best summer was 1953; that was when he scored his only hundred, at Frome (not quite in the Gimblett style there), went on to complete 1,000 runs and earned his cap. As a batsman he could be the most stubborn of grafters, as the Aussies were to discover, but with the ball he was a disappointing successor to Hazell. He later played for Devon.

ROY SMITH Born Taunton, 14.4.30. RHB, SLA. Cap 1953. SFC: 96 matches; 2600 runs @ 17.11; 1 century; HS 100 v Worcestershire, Frome, 1953; 1000 runs once; HT 1176 in 1953; 19 wickets @ 57.00; BB 4-91 v Leicestershire, Leicester, 1952; HT 14 in 1952.

Roy Smith

RICHARD SNELL 1992

He came with the recommendations of Jimmy Cook and David Graveney. But this likeable South African Test all-rounder was never going to be the answer. There was something a little too relaxed in his approach; he lacked the resolve for an arduous season of one-day and three-day matches. It was perhaps significant that his fast-medium never brought more than three wickets in an innings.

RICHARD PETER SNELL Born Durban, South Africa, 12.9.68. RHB, RFM. 3 Tests 1992-. 20 LOI 1991-. SFC: 16 matches; 436 runs @ 27.25; HS 81 v Leicestershire, Grace Road, 1992; 27 wickets @ 44.22; BB 3-29 v Middlesex, Lord's, 1992. NWT: 2 matches; 19 runs @ 19.00; 0 wickets. BHC: 4 matches; 60 runs @ 30.00; 6 wickets @ 29.33. SL: 13 matches; 158 runs @ 31.60; 12 wickets @ 29.92.

JOHN STENTON 1953

Another Yorkshireman who turned up at Taunton — with just one match to show for it. The fact that he bowled left-arm spinners was part of the appeal but his single wicket wasn't sufficient to bring a renewed call.

JOHN DEREK STENTON Born Sheffield, Yorkshire, 26.10.24. RHB, SLA. SFC: 1 match; 19 runs @ 9.50; HS 18 v Surrey, Taunton, 1953; 1 wicket @ 44.00; BB 1-18 same match.

Richard Snell

Haydn Sully

MICHAEL SUTTON — 1948

An Oxford blue just after the war and some useful hauls as an off-spinner were enough to earn him a solitary county appearance (against Oxford, as it happened).

MICHAEL ANTHONY SUTTON Born Weymouth, Dorset, 29.3.21. RHB, OB. SFC: 1 match; 13 runs @ 13.00; HS 13* v Oxford, Bath, **1948**; BB 1-34 same match. Oxford 1946-47.

IAN SWALLOW — 1990 - 1991

Any off-spinner who had been brought in to do what Vic Marks had done so well was going to be subjected to unfair comparisons. He had hoped in vain that a career, which had only flickered with his native Yorkshire, would now be encouragingly relaunched. He was, in fact, a competent slow bowler and one suitably praised at times by Jackie Birkenshaw. But the county came to the conclusion that he wasn't going to take enough wickets.

IAN GEOFFREY SWALLOW Born Barnsley, Yorkshire, 18.12.62. RHB, OB. SFC: 27 matches; 254 runs @ 21.17; HS 41* v Glamorgan, Taunton, 1991; HT 187 in 1990; 42 wickets @ 60.19; BB 3-43 v Sussex, Taunton, 1991; HT 34 in 1990. NWT: 2 matches; 0 wickets. BHC: 9 matches; 31 runs @ 6.20; 6 wickets @ 53.00. SL: 15 matches; 81 runs @ 27.00; 6 wickets @ 63.50. Yorkshire 1983-89.

HAYDN SULLY — 1959 - 1963

It was never going to be easy as an off-break bowler making a mark in a side which already had the experienced Langford. He had only a dozen matches so wisely tried elsewhere. At Northants he took his 100 wickets in 1966, making a point or two at home.

HAYDN SULLY Born Sampford Brett, Somerset, 1.11.39. LHB, ROB. SFC: 12 matches; 98 runs @ 14.00; HS 24 v Gloucestershire, Bath, 1963; 12 wickets @ 46.42; BB 5-64 v Cambridge, Taunton, 1961. Northamptonshire 1964-69.

ROY SULLY — 1985

Useful local cricketer who shaped well at 2nd XI level. His sole Sunday League appearance still came as something of a surprise. Played football for Western League sides including Taunton Town and Barnstaple.

ROYSTON CYRIL JOHN SULLY Born Taunton, 10.4.51. RHB, RM. SL: 1 match; 2 runs @ 2.00; 0 wickets.

Ian Swallow

HAROLD STEPHENSON
1948 - 1964

He stands, statistically alone, as the county's finest
wicketkeeper. One is only saddened that Test
recognition slipped insensitively past him, maybe
because he played only for Somerset or, more
realistically, because of the exceptional wealth of
the competition. The Commonwealth tour to
India and Ceylon in 1950-51 wasn't quite the
same. He came down from the North on the
canny word of Micky Walford, quickly proved
himself as consistent a 'keeper as any in the
country and, as a bonus for the West Country
crowds, specialised gleefully and with
consummate skill in the seemingly suicidal single
during his innate pursuit of quick runs. Indeed
he scored 1,000 runs five times, aided by the
youthful alacrity with which he bounded out of
his ground.

As he crouched behind the stumps, the pads
invariably looked too big for him. But he was a
great technician, with the anticipation and
intuition to take the sorcery or unpredictable
variants of Lawrence. He was a pragmatic rather
than daring captain during his five years in
charge. Under him Somerset came third in the
table and weren't so far off the pennant. The
parting carried certain pangs. He continued to
live in Taunton but didn't return too often to the
County Ground.

Keeping wicket for Dorset, there was still
enough agility in him to suggest that the back was
playing him up less and that Somerset needn't
have been quite so ready to hunt for a successor.
He liked a drink, liked to make quick runs in the
evening sunshine and liked to win without too
much hassle. His loyalty to fellow pros was
apparent; he was inclined to bristle when officials
implied that it was time to bring in wet-behind-
the-ears vacation players. *Photo opposite.*

HAROLD WILLIAM STEPHENSON Born Haverton Hill, County
Durham, 18.7.20. RHB, WK. Cap 1949. Captain 1960-64. SFC: 427
matches; 12473 runs @ 20.02; 7 centuries; HS 147* v
Nottinghamshire, Bath, 1962; 1000 runs 4 times; HT 1085 in 1953; 0
wickets; 1007 dismissals (698 ct, 309 st). GC: 1 match; 4 runs @ 4.00.

Nick Taylor

NICK TAYLOR
1986

So disappointed that he had been released by
Surrey, where coach Geoff Arnold had changed
his fast bowler's action for the better, Taylor went
off to Australia with no thoughts of any more
cricket. He returned, with fresh hopes at
Somerset, yet only to last for one season.
Team-mates found him an individualist. He had
acting aspirations; he'd done sporadic film work
in Australia, had worked as a model, squash
coach, waiter and bouncer. But what he wanted
most of all was to follow successfully the career of
his father, Ken, the Yorkshire and England player.
Nick had actually started with two years on the
Yorkshire staff.

NICHOLAS SIMON TAYLOR Born Holmfirth, Yorkshire, 2.6.63.
RHB, RFM. SFC: 16 matches; 107 runs @ 8.92; HS 24* v
Gloucestershire, Taunton, 1986; 29 wickets @ 42.14; BB 4-40 v
Essex, Taunton, 1986. NWT: 2 matches; 1 run (no average); 5
wickets @ 13.60. BHC: 3 matches; 10 runs @ 5.00; 5 wickets @
22.20. SL: 13 matches; 31 runs @ 10.33; 19 wickets @ 22.21.
Yorkshire 1982-83; Surrey 1984-85.

CHRIS TAVARE
1989 - 1993

He was not an ostentatious express train. It was not his style to court popularity with flamboyant liberties. Indeed some would say that Somerset have had few more introverted skippers. During the course of an innings there was hardly ever a flicker of emotion, not once a nuance of levity. It is possible that he was not a bundle of uninhibited fun in the dressing room. Bad psychology and a meanness of spirit on the part of some of those in charge at Kent meant he was ready to leave. The invitation to Somerset came primarily from his pal, Vic Marks. Down in the West Country, from where his wife hailed after all, there was going to be need of an experienced captain. Tavare was never a man for rash decisions; he chose to come, first as a player and later skipper. That phlegmatic exterior masked a sharp tactical sense. He may have spurned risk and too many flights of imagination but he could be a calculating competitor. There was also ample paradox in his batting. The popular image suggested the obdurate occupant of the crease. In truth, he could emerge as a most fluent and crisp stroke-maker. Note his success-rate in one-day matches — he was capable of pushing the score along comfortably without the hint of a wanton blow. But the summer of 1993 brought him meagre success. The technical assuredness and concentration lessened. Quiet and dignified as ever, he announced his retirement and planned for a career in marketing outside the game.

CHRISTOPHER JAMES TAVARE Born Orpington, Kent, 27.10.54. RHB, RM. Cap 1989. Captain 1990-93. 31 Tests 1980-89. 29 LOI 1980-84. SFC: 102 matches; 6365 runs @ 43.60; 13 centuries; HS 219 v Sussex, Hove, 1990; 1000 runs 4 times; HT 1638 in 1990; 0 wickets. NWT: 13 matches; 747 runs @ 93.38; 0 wickets; MoM 1. BHC: 24 matches; 883 runs @ 46.47; GA 3. SL: 71 matches; 1830 runs @ 29.05. Kent 1974-88; Oxford 1975-77.

GERRY TORDOFF
1950 - 1955

By some means or other, his partial release was obtained from the Royal Navy for a season, so that he could lead Somerset. It was a bad appointment, though the blame should be levelled more at the committee than the skipper. He was a useful left-hand bat, with some powerful shots and three centuries in the first-class game. More experienced players used to say that he was too loose with his batting and would profit from a

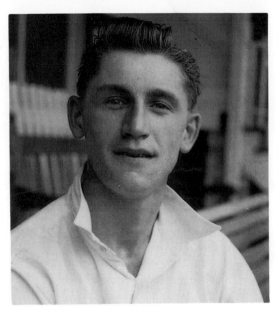

Gerry Tordoff

tighter technique. He passed 1,000 runs, with one memorable fighting innings against Gloucestershire in his year as captain. But it was unreasonable to expect him to come in and lift an undistinguished side. Somerset stayed on the bottom. He probably enjoyed his carefree cricket with Combined Services and Berks far more.

GERALD GEORGE TORDOFF Born Whitwood, Yorkshire, 6.12.29. LHB, RM. Cap 1952. Captain 1955. SFC: 54 matches; 2417 runs @ 25.44; 3 centuries; HS 145* v Gloucestershire, Taunton, 1955; 1000 runs once; HT 1132 in 1955; 26 wickets @ 46.04; BB 4-43 v Northamptonshire, Glastonbury, 1952. Cambridge 1952.

MARCUS TRESCOTHICK
1993 -

England have monitored and recognised his talents at Under-17, Under-18 and, with 'Tests' against the West Indians, at Under-19 level. His schoolboy promise was exceptional and in one extraordinary season he played so many matches and pulverised so many youthful local bowlers that he ended up with more than 4,000 runs. There were big scores for Keynsham, the club for whom his father, Martyn, a well-known cricketer, plays and is the chairman. Marcus's debut for Somerset's senior side in 1993 was hardly dramatic, though runs were plentiful for the 2nd XI.

MARCUS TRESCOTHICK Born Keynsham, Avon, 25.12.75. LHB. SFC; 3 matches; 16 runs @ 2.33; HS 6 v Sussex, Taunton, 1993. SL: 3 matches; 32 runs @ 10.67.

DEREK TAYLOR   1970 - 1982

There are various tests for a top-notch wicketkeeper. How they get on against the off-spinner is the obvious one. But not so far behind is their ability to stand up to the best of the medium-pacers who can make the ball 'wobble' at will. Taylor's proficiency in harness with the brilliant Cartwright was legendary. No-one ever remembered his putting down a catch in the process. The tragedy of Taylor's career was that there were too many great 'keepers around at the same time. He earned his Test trial in 1976 — but for the most time he was destined to be the country's No. 3. And that means nothing. He came from Surrey Seconds and for the next dozen or so years did everything behind the stumps with the minimum of fuss. Just before he left, emigrating to Australia for a new career in insurance, he was creating a new one-day record by taking eight catches against Oxford and Cambridge in the Benson and Hedges. His batting should never be discounted; he knew his limits and kept within them, making himself into a most adequate opening bat when the need was there. In the dressing room, surrounded by more volatile influences, he could be a calming creature. *Photo opposite.*

DEREK JOHN SOMERSET TAYLOR Born Amersham, Buckinghamshire, 12.11.42. RHB, WK. Cap 1971. SFC: 280 matches; 6800 runs @ 22.44; 4 centuries; HS 179 v Glamorgan, Swansea, 1974; 1000 runs once; HT 1121 in 1975; 0 wickets; 661 dismissals (587 ct, 74 st). GC/NWT: 28 matches; 244 runs @ 18.77; BHC: 50 matches; 603 runs @ 31.74; GA 1. SL: 183 matches; 1188 runs @ 16.50. Surrey 1966-69; Griqualand West, South Africa, 1970-72.

Gareth Townsend

GARETH TOWNSEND   1990 - 1992

Clinched his contract on the strength of some impressive scoring in a 2nd XI match. He was described as a battler, capable of occupying the crease. And with the equable temperament you'd expect from a Devonian. Solid ability was always there; but promotion did not come easily and he was released in 1992.

GARETH TERENCE JOHN TOWNSEND Born Tiverton, Devon, 28.6.68. RHB. SFC: 12 matches; 414 runs @ 20.70; HS 53 v Sri Lankans, Taunton, 1991; HT 272 in 1992. BHC: 1 match; 1 run @ 1.00. SL: 3 matches; 87 runs @ 29.00.

Graham Tripp

GRAHAM TRIPP   1955 - 1959

The runs never came as they promised to. Thirty-four matches over five summers offered modest scope for a good-looking bat who always shaped so well in the 2nd XI and in the nets.

GRAHAM MALCOLM TRIPP Born Clevedon, Somerset, 29.6.32. RHB. SFC: 34 matches; 700 runs @ 12.73; HS 62 v Essex, Colchester, 1957; HT 217 in 1956; 0 wickets.

MAURICE TREMLETT 1947 - 1960

Here was Somerset's first professional captain: a social as well as a sporting statement. He did it particularly well for much of the time. Few over the post-war decades had a more acute tactical awareness. He kept games nicely balanced and always tried to persuade the opposition to remain interested. Countering this was an easy-going, even lackadaisical nature. He was often one of the boys, a popular member of the team and much liked around the boundary. But on the occasions when club politics got perniciously to work and he sensed that other candidates for his job might be advocated by some of the committee, he went into a shell.

He started as the office boy at Taunton and quickly acquired something of a golden-boy image when he made his heroic entry at Lord's, to beat Middlesex almost on his own, soon after the war. The premature praise embarrassed him; he was never a conceited man. He was taken to the West Indies, where Gubby Allen persuaded him to lengthen his run-up and experiment with his action in a search for added pace. It was a disaster. The bowler went miserably into decline. At home, he lost length, line and confidence — and simply got on with his batting. The stroke-making could be clean, straight and excitingly lofted, even if inconsistent. He took a fearful blow on the forehead and almost lost an eye when fielding at silly mid-off at Bath. The balance was never the same again. Yet the record reminds us that this fair-haired batsman could score 2,000 runs in a season. He was born in Cheshire but a Somerset lad in every sense. *Photo opposite.*

> **MAURICE FLETCHER TREMLETT** Born Stockport, Cheshire, 5.7.23. RHB, RFM. Cap 1947. Captain 1956-59. 3 Tests 1948. SFC: 353 matches; 15195 runs @ 25.93; 15 centuries; HS 185 v Northamptonshire, Northampton, 1951; 1000 runs 9 times; HT 2071 in 1951; 326 wickets @ 29.04; BB 8-31 v Glamorgan, Weston-super-Mare, 1948; HT 83 in 1948. Central Districts, New Zealand, 1951-52. Died 30.7.84.

HARVEY TRUMP 1988 -

During his year with Somerset, David Graveney was an enthusiastic admirer of Harvey, seeing him as an off-spinner with the natural aggression of a fast bowler. He can be intense and competitive, revealed in the way he takes those return catches. The promise was noted in Millfield days. He captained the county at various schools' levels, and represented England as an Under-15 all-rounder. His introduction to first-class cricket came first as a part-timer as he completed his studies. Against Gloucestershire he took seven wickets in each innings. His father, a schoolmaster, captained Devon. Harvey, who teaches History and PE himself, has the resolve for further progress. The arrival of Mushtaq Ahmed predictably worked against Trump up to a point, limiting his opportunities in 1993.

> **HARVEY RUSSELL JOHN TRUMP** Born Taunton, 11.10.68. RHB, OB. SFC: 73 matches; 508 runs @ 10.16; HS 48 v Nottinghamshire, Taunton, 1988 (debut); HT 154 in 1992; 172 wickets @ 38.28; BB 7-52 (twice) v Gloucestershire, Gloucester, 1992; HT 51 in 1991. NWT: 5 matches; 2 runs @ 1.00; 2 wickets @ 76.50. BHC: 7 matches; 3 runs @ 1.00; 4 wickets @ 49.25. SL: 42 matches; 74 runs @ 10.57; 29 wickets @ 42.38.

Harvey Trump

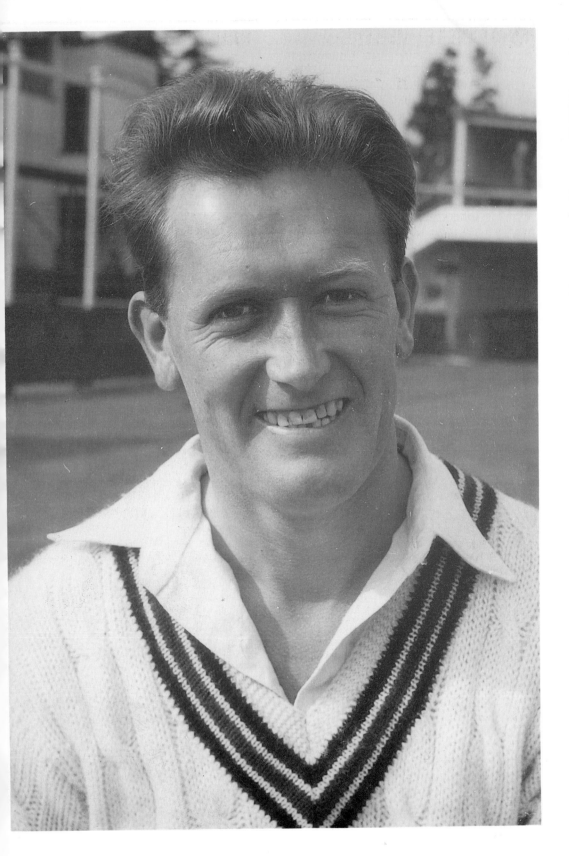

Murray Turner

MURRAY TURNER   1984 - 1986

He was a lively and successful club cricketer in the Taunton area, his progress having been monitored from early schooldays. But in the end there were no more than a dozen first-class matches to show for it. He joined the RAF instead, where he found renewed scope for runs and, more significantly for a quickish bowler, wickets.

MURRAY STEWART TURNER Born Shaftesbury, Dorset, 27.1.64. RHB, RFM. SFC: 12 matches; 144 runs @ 18.00; HS 24* v Warwickshire, Taunton, 1985; 15 wickets @ 52.53; BB 4-74 same match. BHC: 4 matches; 42 runs @ 21.00; 4 wickets @ 39.00. SL: 13 matches; 49 runs @ 9.80; 10 wickets @ 42.10.

ROBERT TURNER   1991 -

After captaining Cambridge and Combined Universities, it was inevitable that back at Taunton he would need patience as No. 2 keeper to Neil Burns. Behind the stumps there was nothing flashy in his style. As a batsman he lacked nothing in application — and was rewarded with a painstaking and determined century against Notts. With Burns apparently out of favour, Turner was brought into the side at Weston-super-Mare in 1993, and stayed there.

ROBERT JULIAN TURNER Born Malvern, Worcestershire, 25.11.67. RHB, WK. SFC: 14 matches; 500 runs @ 35.71; 1 century; HS 101* v Nottinghamshire, Taunton, 1992; HT 287 in 1992; 0 wickets; 17 dismissals (14 ct, 3 st). SL: 6 matches; 71 runs @ 17.75.

Robert Turner

SIMON TURNER   1984 - 1985

From the same talented Weston-super-Mare family as Robert, he displayed the same eagerness (a few years earlier) to try his luck as a county cricketer, and like his brother he was a wicketkeeper of thoroughly sound ability. But really only made his brief appearances when Trevor Gard was injured.

SIMON JONATHAN TURNER Born Cuckfield, Sussex, 28.4.60. LHB, WK. SFC: 6 matches; 84 runs @ 28.00; HS 27* v Glamorgan, Taunton, 1984; 19 dismissals (14 ct, 5 st). NWT: 3 matches; 7 runs @ 7.00. SL: 4 matches; 16 runs @ 16.00.

PAUL UNWIN   1989

Over here on a cricketing exchange scheme. Made his surprise sole entry into first-class cricket, against the Australians, when Vic Marks was not available.

PAUL DAVID UNWIN Born Waipawa, New Zealand, 9.6.67. RHB, OB. SFC: 1 match; 4 runs (no average); HS 4* v Australians, Taunton, 1989; 5 wickets @ 23.20; BB 3-73 same match. Central Districts, New Zealand 1986-.

ANDRE VAN TROOST   1991 -

the fastest bowler in the world seemed a trifle exaggerated. But at times he is very fast indeed and almost unplayable. At his best he is without question a match-winner. He doesn't lack ambition and news that the TCCB weren't prepared to shorten his period of qualification for England came as a big disappointment.

...et no-one discount his pace or his bounce (he's 6ft 7ins, after all). He represented Holland — like his grandfather, who was still playing in his eighties — and came to Somerset at the same time as Roland Lefebvre. He has taken six wickets in an innings more than once and, with the added control that he is striving to acquire, he's capable of making a genuine impact in this country. As for his unconventional batting, that's something else. A conversational aside by Desmond Haynes that Van Troost was arguably

ADRIANUS PELRUS VAN TROOST Born Schiedam, Holland, 2.10.72. RHB, RF. SFC: 29 matches; 150 runs @ 10.00; HS 35 v Lancashire, Taunton, 1993; HT 108 in 1993; 58 wickets @ 35.67; BB 6-48 v Essex, Taunton, 1992; HT 31 in 1993. NWT: 4 matches; 20 runs @ 20.00; 6 wickets @ 27.17. BHC: 2 matches; 9 runs, no average; 2 wickets @ 19.00. SL: 7 matches; 8 runs @ 4.00; 7 wickets @ 27.71.

Tony Vickery

But he was destined to end up 12th man. Roy had grown up near the County Ground, going straight from Huish's Grammar School to the ground-staff. By the age of 20 he had been awarded his cap. Apart from the runs, he fielded well at short-leg, and was a passable wicketkeeper in an emergency. His career with Somerset ended in too many frustrations; he surprised many by moving to Northants for five seasons, briefly captaining them in the process. *Photo opposite.*

ROY THOMAS VIRGIN Born Taunton, 26.8.39. RHB, LB. Cap 1960. SFC: 321 matches; 15458 runs @ 28.52; 22 centuries; HS 179* v Lancashire, Old Trafford, 1971; 1000 runs 9 times; HT 2223 in 1970; 4 wickets @ 80.25; BB 1-6 v Lancashire, Taunton, 1969. GC: 22 matches; 717 runs @ 35.85; 1 wicket @ 1.00; MoM 2. BHC: 3 matches; 33 runs @ 11.00. SL: 59 matches; 1188 runs @ 22.85. Northamptonshire 1973-77; Western Province, South Africa, 1972-73.

TONY VICKERY 1947 - 1948

The medical profession had first call on him. That was the county's loss. Here was a solid, technically skilful batsman, never seen at anything like his best during his sporadic post-war appearances.

ANTHONY VICKERY Born Taunton, 26.8.25. RHB. SFC: 6 matches; 89 runs @ 8.09; HS 21 v Worcestershire, Worcester, 1947.

ROY VIRGIN 1957 - 1972

That 1970 summer belonged to him. There were nine hundreds, seven of them in the championship. The timing never seemed to falter with those exquisite, at times underrated, cover drives of his. Some said his repertoire was inclined to be modest, though he certainly embraced additional forcing shots. This was noticeable in the conscious way he complemented his off-side approach with the occasional hook and improving on-driving. He was smallish, sturdy and always tidy in his batsmanship. And he looked fluent enough — at least in the view of every fellow Tauntonian — in that golden '70 summer of his to book himself a tour place. It didn't come; being first to 2,000 runs and one of Wisden's 'famous five' wasn't quite enough. In 1971 his expectations were high when he was called up, to stand by for the injured Boycott, at Lord's in the final Test against India.

MALCOLM WALKER 1952 - 1958

Like one or two other off-spinners, this Yorkshireman was unlucky enough to be around in the West Country when Brian Langford was making his impact. The frustrating result was that he played fewer than 30 times for his adopted county. He was no slouch with the bat, opening for the 2nd XI and grafting his way to a championship hundred against Essex. His untimely death came in a motor-cycle accident.

MALCOLM WALKER Born Mexborough, Yorkshire, 14.10.33. RHB, OB. SFC: 29 matches; 574 runs @ 11.71; 1 century; HS 100 v Essex, Romford, 1955; HT 251 in 1956; 28 wickets @ 34.86; BB 5-45 v Gloucestershire, Bristol, 1955; HT 12 in 1955. Died August 1986.

Malcolm Walker

MICKY WALFORD 1946 - 1953

Now here was undeniable class. He would arrive in August, straight from his teaching duties at Sherborne, to compile his centuries and play with a stylish orthodoxy and grace that brought murmurs of jealousy from one of two established heroes. His fiercely competitive nature probably came from his North Country roots; he wasn't gregarious and was seen by some of the pros as a cold fish. But his eloquence at the wicket was a rare and cherished joy. Surely, if he had been available more often for county cricket, he'd have walked into the Test team.

He scored a hundred, undefeated, on his Somerset debut. The vacations coincided with Weston, and that was where he fashioned six of his centuries. His technique, with the sweetest of strokes off the front and back foot through the covers, was a delightful lesson to every schoolboy who came to watch. In a ham-fisted and tactless approach, for reasons that are not apparent, Somerset finally asked him if he'd be prepared to surrender his special registration so that they could use it for someone else. He would have gone on for another season or two.

Micky could have played part-time for Warwickshire. After meeting RJO Meyer and an exchange of letters, he chose Somerset instead — because of its proximity to Sherborne. In turn, Walford recommended Harold Stephenson to Somerset. He was a fine all-round sportsman; quite apart from his considerable gifts as an opening bat, he was an outstanding centre three-quarter who played in final England trials and in wartime internationals, while he represented his country at hockey. *Photo opposite.*

MICHAEL MOORE WALFORD Born Stockton-on-Tees, County Durham, 27.11.15. Cap 1946. RHB, SLA. SFC: 52 matches; 3393 runs @ 40.90; 7 centuries; HS 264 v Hampshire, Weston-super-Mare, 1947; HT 942 in 1947; 1 wicket @ 71.00; BB 1-18 v Lancashire, Weston-super-Mare, 1952. Oxford 1935-38.

HUGH WATTS 1939 - 1952

Who said that Somerset stuck to three captains in the bizarre leadership machinations of 1948? Watts was No. 4 — against Hants at Bath — and there were others. He used to be a history master at Downside, and got dubbed 'The Abbot' by some of the pros because of it. War wounds curbed his talents as an all-rounder. He was a

Hugh Watts

popular team-mate and, at times, a most attractive left-hander whose only championship hundred came against Glamorgan when Len Muncer got in a bit of a strop because of criticism from Wilf Wooller and started bowling full tosses as Watts moved into the 90s. His spectacles gave him a studious appearance.

HUGH EDMUND WATTS Born Stratton-on-the-Fosse, Somerset, 4.3.22. LHB, RLB. SFC: 61 matches; 2511 runs @ 25.11; 1 century; HS 110 v Glamorgan, Weston-super-Mare, 1949; HT 543 in 1947; 0 wickets. Cambridge 1947.

GILES WHITE 1991 -

Has shaped well for Devon as an all-rounder. The fact that he's a leg-spinner generates added interest, but the presence of Mushtaq Ahmed made recognition for White more difficult. Ability was keenly monitored from Millfield days; then came Loughborough University.

GILES WILLIAM WHITE Born Barnstaple, Devon, 23.3.72. RHB, LB. SFC: 1 match; 42 runs @ 42.00; HS 42 v Sri Lankans, Taunton, 1992; 1 wicket @ 30.00; BB 1-30 same match. SL: 3 matches; 41 runs @ 13.67.

e followed Martin Crowe, as Somerset sustained ieir envied reputation for enticing talented verseas players. As a batsman he could ffortlessly adapt his approach to the needs of the :am. The style could be decidedly handsome, ith more fluent off-side shots than one sees from ianyAustralians. He was at his best when eagerly ooking for runs; they came from the sharpness of ie eye and the elegance of the wrist. Matches ere for winning; the stern expression on the face evealed his Antipodean origins and his hilosophy for the game. He was in tremendous orm for Somerset in 1988, heading the national verages and causing people to realise why one or vo respected pundits at home were comparing im with McCabe. Everyone, including Waugh, greed that the relative tranquillity of the West ountry suited his temperament and made him a iore relaxed batsman.

STEPHEN RODGER WAUGH Born Sydney, Australia, 2.6.65. RHB, RMF. Cap 1988. 58 Tests 1985-. 147 LOI 1986-. SFC: 19 matches; 1654 runs @ 78.76; 8 centuries; HS 161 v Kent, Canterbury, 1988; 1000 runs once; HT 1314 in 1988; 14 wickets @ 29.14; BB 3-48 v Surrey, Oval, 1987. NWT: 2 matches; 21 runs @ 10.50; 4 wickets @ 24.00. BHC: 3 matches; 161 runs @ 80.50; 2 wickets @ 31.50; GA 1. SL: 11 matches; 534 runs @ 66.75; 2 wickets @ 57.00. New South Wales, Australia, 1984-.

teve Waugh

In 1938 he took 172 wickets, more than anyone else. He did it with a much-imitated leap just before releasing the ball, genuine pace and consistent swing away from the batsman. Yet, in the perverse ways of cricketing lore, the majority of the stories about him concern his batting. For he was a slogger, glorious, with a pragmatic method distilled from the muscular orthodoxy of a hundred Somerset meadows (though he came from Kent himself). He would also claim that his many sixes, which in total made up virtually a quarter of all his runs for the county, were for the most part straight and scientifically dispatched. In truth, they described a wildish arc, threatened to get lost in the clouds and ended up — as authentically detailed — in distant allotments or passing trains.

He first turned up in Somerset, with what then seemed like a Cockney accent and flashy suit, to become an instant idol among the less sophisticated members of the staff. They admired his varying skills with ball and bat, just as they did the way he could regularly win a trick at cards or follow the right dog in the evening meeting straight after the close of play. His image was made for Somerset; in return he served them well and a more sensitive county would have kept him on for another year or so at the end. He played only two Tests, against New Zealand in 1937 and Australia the following summer. He'd have gone to India but for the war. Later, as some of the venom went out of his bowling, he turned more to his off-breaks. He was still able to take those blinding catches at silly mid-off. Doting third-formers came to chuckle at his exploits, and return the ball from the French beans. Rowing boats were at hand to retrieve from the adjacent Tone. Harold Pinter eulogised him in print and even persuaded an ageing Arthur to play for the showbizzy Gaieties CC. *Photo opposite.*

ARTHUR WILLIAM WELLARD Born Southfleet, Kent, 8.4.02. RHB, RFM/OB. Cap 1929. 2 Tests 1937-38. SFC: 391 matches; 11432 runs @ 19.34; 2 centuries; HS 112 v Surrey, Oval, 1934, and v Lancashire, Old Trafford, 1935; 1000 runs twice; HT 1232 in 1935; Double — twice in 1933, 1935; 1517 wickets @ 24.32; BB 8-52 v Worcestershire, Bath, 1947; 100 wickets 8 times; HT 169 in 1938. Died 31.12.80.

Alan Whitehead

ALAN WHITEHEAD 1957 - 1961

n the opinion of many, he's one of our best
umpires. But he suffered unfairly, some would
argue, because of a moment or two of controversy.
He's old-fashioned, a stickler, not prepared to be
bullied. In his five years as a slow left-arm bowler for
Somerset, his appearances were intermittent and he
never found the scope to build on a particularly
memorable stint at Eastbourne. The county were
searching for Hazell's successor, and they decided
that Whitehead didn't have enough variety or
penetration. It was all anti-climax after a debut at 16.

ALAN GEOFFREY THOMAS WHITEHEAD Born Butleigh,
Somerset, 28.10.40. LHB, SLA. SFC: 38 matches; 137 runs @ 5.71;
HS 15 v Hampshire, Southampton, 1959; 67 wickets @ 34.42; BB
6-74 v Sussex, Eastbourne, 1959; HT 44 in 1959. Fc umpire 1970-.

PETER WIGHT 1953 - 1965

Who said he didn't relish fast bowling? You
should have seen him taking on the speed
merchants in 1960. Well yes, he did occasionally
appear to have a problem or two against Trueman
— and it was even interpreted as fear. But this
slim, almost delicate batsman could parade an
exquisite and seemingly intrepid repertoire of
forcing shots, often when one of the openers had
gone and the shine wasn't off the ball. He'd come
to England to play some league cricket for
Burnley and he was a natural for the transition to
the county game.

Those 27 hundreds were laden with the riches
of his crisp driving, or the square-cutting when he
went up onto his toes. He could hit on the up
with a distinctive freedom. His first match for
Somerset had been against the Australians, who
very quickly got him caught in the slips in the
opening innings. Wight was rarely a man of
emotion but he was privately imagining that his
first-class career was coming to the hastiest of
conclusions when Richie Benaud said: "Cheer up,
you'll get a hundred in the second innings." And
he did. In the dressing room he could look
nervous and morose, worrying about suspect
health and fitness. All signs of such neuroses were
forgotten once he got to the crease. At his best he
was a brilliant bat; he might have turned into a
successful off-spinner with more overs (and
confidence to go with them). Once at
Chesterfield, Stephenson threw the ball to him
and he picked up a perfunctory six wickets. After
his playing days came the success of his indoor
school at Bath, and his first-class umpiring.
Photo opposite.

PETER BERNARD WIGHT Born Georgetown, British Guiana,
25.6.30. RHB, OB. Cap 1954. SFC: 321 matches; 16965 runs @
32.75; 27 centuries; HS 222* v Kent, Taunton, 1959; 1000 runs 10
times; HT 2316 in 1960; 62 wickets @ 33.24; BB 6-29 v Derbyshire,
Chesterfield, 1957; HT 12 in 1958. GC: 6 matches; 56 runs @ 9.33.
British Guiana, West Indies, 1950-51; Canterbury, New Zealand,
1963-64. Fc umpire 1966-.

STEVE WILKINSON 1972 - 1974

Nice-looking
bat without
being dominant
enough. Once
earned an
unlikely rebuke
from skipper
Close: "You play
too straight,
lad." That was
after Wilkinson
had played the
ball back and
got Close run-out at the other end. Around for
three years but the breakthrough proved elusive.

STEPHEN GEORGE WILKINSON Born Hounslow, Middlesex, 12.1.49.
RHB, SLA. SFC: 18 matches; 452 runs @ 20.55; HS 69 v Surrey, Oval,
1972; HT 299 in 1972; 0 wickets. GC: 1 match; 5 runs @ 5.00. BHC: 6
matches; 70 runs @ 14.00. SL: 18 matches; 252 runs @ 18.00.

TERRY WILLETTS
1964 - 1967

Close to establishing himself both as a professional cricketer and footballer. His value, as a left-hander, was mostly confined to the 2nd XI. But everyone remembers those sharp reflexes as he fielded close to the wicket.

FRANK TERENCE WILLETTS Born Birmingham, 20.11.39. LHB. SFC: 16 matches; 333 runs @ 11.10; HS 38 v Glamorgan, Weston-super-Mare, 1965; HT 165 in 1965. GC: 3 matches; 27 runs @ 9.00.

LLOYD WILLIAMS
1955

A housemaster at Millfield, he came into the county side during the vacations for just one season. He was a competent bat, scored plenty of runs at club level and captained Bath CC in 1958-59.

GWYNFOR LLOYD WILLIAMS Born Kidwelly, Carmarthenshire, 30.5.25. RHB. SFC: 3 matches; 30 runs @ 5.00; HS 24 v Glamorgan, Weston-super-Mare, 1955.

HUGH WILSON
1983 - 1984

The cruel, unreasonable moment of truth came for him on the day he was inexplicably left out of the NatWest quarter-final side against Kent. He had come, by way of Surrey, big of build and brisk of pace, and probably deserved more overs from Somerset.

PETER HUGH L'ESTRANGE WILSON Born Guildford, Surrey, 17.8.58. RHB, RFM. SFC: 15 matches; 60 runs @ 10.00; HS 25 v Gloucestershire, Bristol, 1983; 30 wickets @ 33.77; BB 4-77 v Gloucestershire, Bath, 1983; HT 25 in 1983. NWT: 2 matches; 2 wickets @ 31.50. BHC: 3 matches; 0 runs; 5 wickets @ 19.60. SL: 8 matches; 2 runs (no average); 7 wickets @ 39.57. Surrey 1978-82; Northern Transvaal, South Africa, 1979-80.

RAYMOND WINDSOR
1969

Here was a prodigious scorer for Wellington and Taunton, who also built a substantial innings of nearly 150 in the 2nd XI against Cornwall. Recognition was scant at the higher level; one appearance, with neither the chance to bat nor bowl.

RAYMOND THOMAS ALBERT WINDSOR Born Wellington, Somerset, 9.2.43. RHB. SFC: 1 match; 0 runs. SL: 1 match; did not bat or bowl.

George Woodhouse

GEORGE WOODHOUSE
1946 - 1953

He was Somerset's youngest captain, at 23, when he first shared the duties in 1948. Then, with quiet efficiency, he did it for a whole season before devoting his time and energies to the family brewery business. He played wartime cricket and rugby for Cambridge. But after his brief, happy spell with Somerset, he accepted that there had to be priorities outside the game. He

as chairman of the Blandford-based Hall & Woodhouse up to the time of his death from a heart attack. In his time he was High Sheriff and Deputy Lieutenant of Dorset. He was a life member of Somerset and was for a time president of Dorset CCC. There were glimpses of his true batting form when he composed his sole century at Leicester.

GEORGE EDWARD SEALEY WOODHOUSE Born Blandford, Dorset, 15.2.24. RHB. Cap 1947. Joint Captain 1948, Captain 1949. SFC: 58 matches; 1903 runs @ 20.68; 1 century; HS 109 v Leicestershire, Leicester, 1947; HT 841 in 1949; 1 wicket @ 8.00; BB 1-8 v Sussex, Eastbourne, 1948. Died 19.1.88.

BOB WOOLSTON 1987

One of the many tried, through the 1960s and after, as a left-arm spinner. He came via the Lord's ground staff. Two expensive wickets were his fleeting reward.

ROBERT GEORGE WOOLSTON Born Enfield, Middlesex, 23.5.68. RHB, SLA. SFC: 1 match; 0 runs; 2 wickets @ 53.50; BB 2-70 v Derbyshire, Taunton, 1987.

Julian Wyatt

JULIAN WYATT 1983 - 1989

His heart belonged to Somerset and, a season or two after he was released, he was back officially as schools coach. He was a farmer's son, who worked ceaselessly to iron out technical flaws. In fact, he was neat and conscientious, whether at the crease or darting around in the field. There were attractive, unflurried strokes which he brought out discriminately during his three centuries. Plenty of courage, too, as demonstrated in a notable innings against the West Indian pacemen.

JULIAN GEORGE WYATT Born Paulton, Somerset, 19.6.63. RHB, RM. SFC: 69 matches; 2789 runs @ 25.35; 3 centuries; HS 145 v Oxford, The Parks, 1985; HT 816 in 1985; 3 wickets @ 32.33; BB 1-0 v Sussex, Hove, 1984. NWT: 4 matches; 20 runs @ 5.00. BHC: 6 matches; 138 runs @ 23.00. SL: 33 matches; 565 runs @ 20.17.

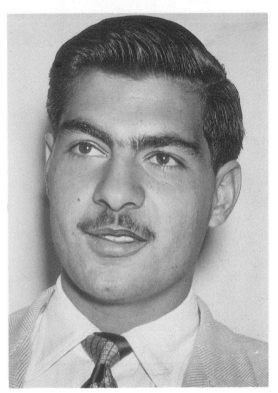

Yawar Saeed

YAWAR SAEED 1953 - 1955

Well-connected in cricketing terms at home. His application was irresistible to Somerset as they sustained their sporting links with the sub-continent. Slightly above medium-pace with the appearance of being faster. Went home to play for Punjab and became a member of the Pakistan Test selection panel.

YAWAR SAEED Born Lahore, India, 22.1.35. RHB, RM. Cap 1954. SFC: 50 matches; 1358 runs @ 15.61; HS 64 v Northamptonshire, Northampton, 1954, and v Middlesex, Bath, 1955; HT 731 in 1955; 78 wickets @ 35.73; BB 5-61 v South Africans, Taunton, 1955; HT 43 in 1955. Punjab, India, 1953-59.